Praise for
Practical Negotiating:
Tools, Tactics, and Techniques

"*Practical Negotiating* is an innovative, resourceful, and—as its name implies—*practical* guide to the art and science of negotiating. Unlike many books on negotiating, which are filled with theories and anecdotes, this one is rich with examples, tactics, and tips, which makes it *the* indispensable book when you are going into any negotiation."

> Terry R. Bacon
> President, Lore International Institute and author of *What People Want: A Manager's Guide to Building Relationships That Work*

"There is something in this book for the most experienced negotiator and the novice. Tom's no nonsense prescriptions and recommendations will hit home. Bound to give you some new ideas for the most difficult of negotiating situations. Anyone in the business world will want this great bible of effective negotiating right near their desk and phone!"

> Dr. Beverly Kaye
> CEO/Founder: Career Systems International
> Coauthor, *Love 'Em or Lose 'Em: Getting Good People to Stay*

"Gosselin has written a thoughtful, engaging, and practical guide on a topic of increasing importance to leaders and organizations. There is something here for anyone who wants to learn how to deal more effectively with the inevitable conflicts that occur in working with clients, customers, and colleagues."

> Peter Cairo, PhD
> Partner, Mercer Delta Consulting
> Coauthor, *Why CEOs Fail* and *Head, Heart, & Guts*

"Forget the image of negotiation being a battlefield. Tom guides you in the development of a road map so both sides become winners and leave the table victorious. Tom's writing is just like his training—clear, concise, and practical. You can apply the process immediately. A handbook for life. Practical, thoughtful, insightful."

> Steven Myers
> Manager, Lighting Education and Sales Training
> Philips Lighting Company

"Skip the workshops and buy *Practical Negotiating*. After field-testing the content through decades of experience, Gosselin has packed this useful book with processes that work and great questions and worksheets that force the material to become real and personal. *Practical Negotiating* will change your thinking about negotiating, and more importantly, will change your behavior. Highly recommended."

> Steve Hopkins
> Publisher, *Executive Times*

"Tom is a most articulate and engaging businessman, and this, coupled with a keen intellect and sharp observation of behavior (and a great sense of humor!) make this a 'must read.' His deep understanding of effective models of negotiation, and their practical application make him one of the leaders in this field."

> Keith G. Slater
> Past Director of International Development, Ingersoll Rand

"The best and most comprehensive description of the negotiation process that I have seen. Clearly written, plenty of pertinent real-life examples, and applicable to any negotiating situation."

> David E. Berlew, PhD
> Former faculty member, Sloan School of Management, MIT
> Cofounder and CEO of McBer & Company (now Hay-McBer)
> and Situation Management Systems, Inc.
> Former CEO of Rath and Strong, Inc.

"This book is aptly titled as it provides the practical "how to" for planning and executing effective negotiations. It's rich with examples, exercises, and reusable tools."

> Dr. Rita Smith
> Dean, Ingersoll Rand University
> Board Member, ASTD

PRACTICAL
TOOLS, TACTICS, & TECHNIQUES
NEGOTIATING

Tom Gosselin

BICENTENNIAL
1807
WILEY
2007
BICENTENNIAL

John Wiley & Sons, Inc.

Published by John Wiley & Sons, Inc., Hoboken, New Jersey.
Published simultaneously in Canada.

Wiley Bicentennial Logo: Richard J. Pacifico

For general information on our other products and services or for technical support, please contact our Customer Care Department within the United States at (800) 762-2974, outside the United States at (317) 572-3993 or fax (317) 572-4002.

Wiley also publishes its books in a variety of electronic formats. Some content that appears in print may not be available in electronic books. For more information about Wiley products, visit our web site at www.wiley.com.

Library of Congress Cataloging-in-Publication Data:

Gosselin, Tom, 1948-
  Practical negotiating : tools, tactics & techniques / Tom Gosselin.
      p.   cm.
  Includes bibliographical references.
  ISBN 978-0-470-13485-6 (cloth)
  1. Negotiation in business.   2. Negotiation.   I. Title.
HD58.6.G665 2007
658.4'052—dc22

                                                2007000457

Printed in the United States of America.

10 9 8 7 6 5 4 3 2 1

To Renee, Cameron, and Travis for their love and support.
And to Fred A. Beaty, my wonderful father-in-law
who taught all of them how to negotiate.

Contents

CONTENTS

Contents

Acknowledgments

This book is not a one-person effort by far. I am especially indebted to my wife Renee Beaty who not only put up with me during the ups and downs of writing but who also did a superb job of copyediting and graphic design. I could not have done this book without her.

In addition, there are specific people who have encouraged, cajoled, shared ideas and stories, and been just plain supportive during the entire process:

- David Berlew, colleague and friend at Situation Management Systems who became my first teacher and mentor when it came to the subject of negotiation.
- Alex Moore and Earl Rose, also of Situation Management Systems, who taught me a great deal during a difficult negotiation.
- Ming Russell, agent and expeditor for this project and I hope others as well.
- Shannon Vargo, associate editor at John Wiley and Sons.
- Bill McCormick, my business partner at the Catalyst Group with whom I collaborated to create much of this material in a workshop setting.
- Mickey and Eleanor McGongale, dedicated public servants who shared their experience in various negotiations that took place in the public sector.

ACKNOWLEDGMENTS

- Steven Myers, client and friend whose encouragement and good humor helped me in so many ways.
- Terry Bacon, of Lore International who encouraged me directly and inspired by example in writing and publishing.
- Jim Kouzes, who gave me the low-down on what kind of commitment a book would take and some great advice for dealing with publishers.

Thank you all for believing in this project and for your help and inspiration in bringing it to fruition.

The Need for Negotiation

Negotiating opportunities surround us.

—R. J. Laser

Conflict in Our Lives

Conflict is inevitable; therefore, negotiation is a survival skill. From the sandbox to the Sinai, every Dick, Jane, Mohammed, and Moshe needs a method to reach workable agreements or suffer the consequences of unresolved conflicts. Whenever one individual's needs, wants, and desires conflict with another's, we have the potential for negotiation. For most of us, 90 percent of the resources we need to do our jobs and live our lives are owned by someone else. Pick up any newspaper and, on the front page, there are numerous examples of conflict situations. To begin, let's define the terms *conflict* and *negotiation:*

Conflict: A situation where two or more parties have interests or perceptions that differ.

Negotiation: A process of exchange to resolve conflict and reach a mutually beneficial agreement.

Consider the number of conflict situations any person experiences in his or her life. From early childhood, we recognize conflict as a part of life:

"I want that."
"No, it's mine."

"I want to ride on Daddy's shoulders!"
"But it's my turn!"

"I want the window seat!"
"So does your sister."

2

Later, conflict may involve disputes about being included in peer groups or competing to be captain of a team. In adulthood, we want to purchase houses, cars, and other items to meet our needs; and many conflicts arise with the significant other in our life. If not handled well, relationships deteriorate and couples divorce. Without a doubt, we encounter many conflicts throughout our lives.

How do we resolve these conflicts? As we grow and mature, we learn to share, compromise, or suspend fulfillment of our needs. We often turn to reason as a method to resolve differences. We reason with the neighbor about the barking dog or overhanging tree branch, but often discover the limits of logic and try to compromise, usually resulting in an unfulfilling solution. Even though these are ways of solving the problem, none involves truly getting our needs met.

In some instances, we depend on the skills of others to help us resolve conflict. When we lack the skills, or the parties involved cannot resolve the conflict, we engage others to explore the issues and reach agreement. These methods have names that include the "-tion" words: *mediation*, *arbitration*, or *litigation*. In the end, the parties expend time and money, and become aggravated, before finally settling a dispute. At that point, the relationship between the parties is often strained or destroyed. To both meet our needs and sustain relationships, *negotiation* becomes the preferred method for reaching agreements. Especially when the exchange is friendly, we may not even realize that we are negotiating as we solve everyday problems, ask for what we want, and make group decisions.

Why is negotiation the preferred method? First, both parties maintain control of the process. Second, if done well, the negotiation can strengthen the relationship between the parties and lead to a deeper understanding and respect—especially, if a long-term relationship is desirable.

Negotiation involves continued interaction and dialogue between parties to find a solution with maximum advantages to both. By negotiation, mutual interests are met and the most satisfactory solution is achieved. However, a negotiation is not a negotiation when one of the parties is powerless, politically, psychologically, or physically, to say no. If you can't say no, call the situation hopeless but don't call it a negotiation.

Conflict inside Organizations

One of the most significant arenas for generating conflict is the workplace. As organizations become less hierarchical and more cross-functional, managers as well as individuals are under increased pressure to resolve conflicts. Interdependence and collaboration are increasingly important issues of nearly everyone's work life. Despite the benefits that accrue from working together, one problem that emerges is the increased likelihood of conflict. Interdependence between individuals and departments with diverse interests and points of view can lead to better results precisely *because* it forces us to deal with the conflicts.

Other trends in business such as lean manufacturing, downsizing, and increased competition for resources also contribute to the increasing frequency of conflict.

Nonproductive Reactions to Conflict

How do people in organizations react to conflict? Some adopt a strategy of denial, choosing to ignore the conflict or pretend that it doesn't exist. They assert that conflict shouldn't exist in organizations because we all share the same goals and objectives. After all, aren't we on the same side?

Most people don't enjoy dealing with conflict, so another common reaction is escalation to a higher authority. Let someone else resolve it. Still another reaction is to capitulate and give in whenever conflict arises. This occurs when someone values peacekeeping more than his or her own needs and desires. One of most insidious reactions is the passive-aggressive response, where the conflict goes underground. The person or group tacitly *agrees* to a change, yet continues to operate as usual—all smiles, no commitment.

Ignoring the conflict, escalating to higher authority, giving in, and responding passive-aggressively are not productive ways to deal with conflict. The underlying issues aren't resolved, relationships are usually strained, agreements aren't honored, and time is wasted. In this book, I explore some productive ways to deal with conflict. If you acknowledge that conflict is inevitable, then learning how to manage conflict well is critical to your success. New leaders especially need negotiation skills: "New leaders fail at an impressive rate. That's because many don't know how to negotiate what they need to improve their odds for success."[1] The challenge for managers and employees involves learning how to resolve conflict, not to minimize or ignore it. This requires negotiation.

Conflict with Customers

Conflict in the arena of sales, and the relationship between the supplier and the customer, deserves special consideration. Most salespeople tend to think of themselves as good negotiators because they have numerous opportunities to negotiate with customers. In workshops with salespeople over the years, their classic dilemmas usually involve two questions:

1. When do I stop selling and start negotiating?
2. How do I avoid giving away too much to make the sale?

The answer to these questions is not simple. Throughout the sales cycle, the supplier and customer have different expectations. As the salesperson works to manage the expectations of the buyer, conflict often arises. Figure 1.1 shows the typical sales cycle.[2]

Consider each of the boxes as a milestone in the sales process. Getting the customer's *attention* requires expending marketing resources. Once the customer has enough *interest* in the product or service to spend some time exploring possibilities with a salesperson, we engage in selling. During the selling process (i.e., determining needs and presenting benefits), the salesperson and customer determine whether there is a good match between needs and product or service.

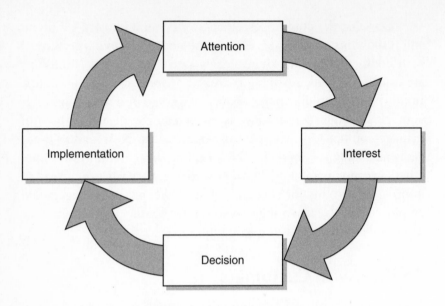

FIGURE 1.1 The Sales Cycle

The ideal outcome is a *decision* in favor of the supplier and a commitment to draw up a contract or agreement toward *implementation*.

Conflict arises in several areas. First, the customer has competing demands for his or her *attention*. Second, the customer wants the supplier to start making concessions early (i.e., between *interest* and *decision*), while the supplier attempts to hold firm until after the *decision* has been made and other suppliers are eliminated. We hear salespeople complain:

> "The customer really holds all the cards."
> "I know my customers pit us against our competitors. I feel like we have to say yes just to stay in the running."

Finally, conflict surfaces in customer situations that involve the interaction of the salesperson as an advocate for the customer with his or her company. This phenomenon is best represented by the equation:

$$1\,\text{External negotiated agreement} = 3\,\text{Internal negotiations}$$

For every external negotiated agreement with a customer, count on at least three internal negotiations required to make the deal work. Picture this: You've just made a deal for a major piece of business with a new customer. Now you have to fight for the resources to make it happen, such as pricing, delivery, credit and payment terms, technical support, and others. Once the deal is done with the customer, the salesperson's internal negotiating has just begun. Chapter 11 covers specific techniques to handle internal negotiations.

Process of Exchange

In the earlier definition of negotiation, I used the phrase *process of exchange*. In the varied ways we exchange currencies for goods and services, negotiation is only one of several processes of exchange. Figure 1.2 represents a hierarchy of the exchange processes based on level of power.

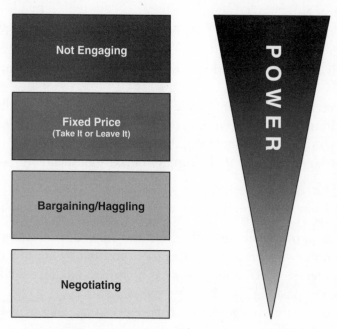

FIGURE 1.2   **Process of Exchange and Power**

At the top of the power scale, the *not engaging* strategy involves a refusal to even open the negotiation. Consider the example of a person who owns a beautiful art object with so much value or meaning to the individual that it's not on the market. Along comes a buyer willing to pay such an outrageous price that the other party is stunned into at least consideration of selling. However, the power lies with the person who owns the object and does not want to sell.

Consider the folksy story of the driver who comes across a beautiful seaside home. The home owner is working in her garden as the potential buyer approaches.

POTENTIAL BUYER: Good afternoon. What a beautiful house you have here.

HOME OWNER: Why thank you, it's been in my family for generations.

POTENTIAL BUYER: Is it for sale?

HOME OWNER: No. There's no way I would ever sell this house.

POTENTIAL BUYER: I would give you $500,000 for it. (Close to market value.)

HOME OWNER: Perhaps you didn't hear me the first time. It's not for sale!

POTENTIAL BUYER: I could increase my offer to $1 million.

HOME OWNER: I wouldn't sell this house for $10 million!

POTENTIAL BUYER: Would you consider $20 million?

HOME OWNER: Well, I guess I'd be foolish not to *consider* that offer.

As you can see, the initial strategy of *not engaging* may be overcome by an overwhelming offer from the other side. However, the home owner displays a very high power position by her unwillingness to engage. The home owner has no *need* to sell, representing a high power position.

The next exchange option is *fixed price* (i.e., take-it-or-leave-it). Most American retail trade is based on this process. The price is established and customers are faced with the decision of whether to buy. This is considered a relatively high power position because the seller has more options (other customers), who are willing to pay the listed price. The advantage of such an approach involves efficiency. Can you image what would happen if every person shopping for groceries engaged in a negotiation for each item in the store? The produce would go bad and the ice cream would melt even before they loaded it into the car. The level of power is contingent on the retailer's belief that "if you don't buy it, someone else will." This stance represents a knowledgeable assessment of the number of potential buyers willing to pay the retailer's price. Retailers do run sales in which they discount from the list price; however, this discount represents a unilateral approach to all buyers, rather than a negotiation with a specific individual.

I first learned about negotiating from my father and uncle in Boston's famous Haymarket. With the wide variety of sidewalk vendors selling the same produce, we could often pit one against the other and get better prices. Our other strategy involved waiting. As the Saturday afternoon sun began to set, we could push prices down even further as the number of customers dwindled. Fixed price depends on the pressure that other buyers are willing to pay the asking price. Consider what happens in a gas crisis when prices are high and supply appears to be low. Drivers will pay the high price believing they have no choice or that prices may rise even further. Couple this with the occasional dwindling supply and anxious consumers will pay dearly to ensure a full tank.

Bargaining, a third process of exchange, involves two parties arguing or haggling over a single currency, usually price, as in the following example:

> BUYER: This copy machine looks like it will meet my needs. How much is it?
>
> SELLER: That machine is $5,000 with a one-year warranty on parts and service.
>
> BUYER: That's more than I have budgeted. How about $3,500?
>
> SELLER: That just would not work for us. Let's say $4,500.

BUYER: How about we split the difference—$4,000?
SELLER: Done!

Most of us are familiar with bargaining and consider it negotiating. But the real distinction between the two involves the use of multiple currencies in negotiating. Let's take the copy machine example and change the dialogue slightly:

BUYER: This copy machine looks like it will meet my needs. How much is it?
SELLER: That machine is $5,000 with a one-year warranty on parts and service.
BUYER: That's more than I have budgeted. How about $3,500?
SELLER: Tell me more about your budget. Have you considered the operating costs in that figure? There's paper, toner, and other supplies. In addition, our maintenance contract is 10 percent of the initial price per year.
BUYER: I hadn't really considered paper, toner, maintenance, or other costs. What can you do for me on that?
SELLER: How about if we offer you a two-year warranty and free toner for a year. In addition, we'll give you the maintenance contract free for the first year, if you pay full price.
BUYER: That's better for our budget. But it still won't work at the $5,000 price.
SELLER: Given your budget constraints, how about leasing the machine for two years and we'll give you a buy-out provision so you can purchase it at the end of the lease. Will that help with your budget?
BUYER: That might work very well. Let's work up the figures and get this going.

Besides price, the seller introduced several other currencies—extending the warranty, free toner, lease versus buy option, and maintenance contract. Once additional currencies are on the table, the parties are freer to mix and match to make the deal more interesting, as well as to meet additional needs for both sides.

Negotiation is the process of exchange that provides the highest likelihood of satisfying the needs of both parties. As in the previous example, the seller was able to generate revenue by leasing the machine. The buyer gained by paying less initially while maintaining the right to purchase at the end of the lease. The other issues of paper, toner, and maintenance fees would be worked out in the negotiation, but consider how much more there is to work with at the end of that meeting than at the beginning.

Introduction to Planning and Executing the Negotiation

This book is organized into two major sections (1) *Planning the Negotiation* and (2) *Executing the Negotiation.*

Overview of Section One: Planning the Negotiation

As a result of reading Section One, you learn to:

- *Identify and satisfy the underlying needs of both sides:* Identifying and satisfying the underlying needs of all parties is at the very heart of good negotiating. Many times, people fail to distinguish between wants and needs. In Chapter 2, you learn more about the distinction between wants and needs, and become more skillful at identifying and satisfying underlying needs—both yours and the other party's.

- *Develop negotiating objectives and establish a position:* Successful negotiators are not only aware of their wants and needs, but also use this information to develop their objectives and plan their position. In Chapter 3, you explore how to distinguish between *business* (or substantive) objectives and *personal* objectives. By converting these objectives into a *position,* you can then build a *settlement range* that includes your opening position, desired settlement point, and walk-away point.

- *Become more skillful and creative at using currencies and concessions:* The concept of exchange—the give-and-take of various currencies or resources—is an integral part of the process of negotiation. After the underlying needs and interests of all parties have been identified, the next step is to explore and exchange currencies or resources that will satisfy the needs of each. Chapter 4 opens your eyes to a plethora of possibilities that make the process of negotiating more interesting and enriching for both parties.

- *Assess your power in negotiation situations:* Many people faced with a negotiation situation underestimate their power simply because they are not aware of their options. Consequently, they may adopt a one-down position and be too willing to make concessions. Others may overestimate their power, act aggressively, and face a lose-lose outcome. The simple rule, "Power is a function of alternatives," will provide you with an easy method to assess and increase your power in negotiating.

Overview of Section Two: Executing the Negotiation

As a result of reading Section Two, you learn:

- *A model for the process of negotiating that has stages and critical tasks:* Although every negotiation is different, successful negotiators tend to follow a certain road map through the three stages of negotiation: (1) opening, (2) exploring, and (3) closing. In each stage, the negotiating process involves critical tasks and behaviors. In Chapter 6, each stage is explained, detailing what you can do to improve your competence at executing each of the critical tasks. As with any model or technology, *simplicity ensures accessibility*. What's the benefit of a complex multiple-step process if you can't remember it or follow the process easily?

- *To identify your negotiating style and become more flexible in using various skills:* By taking a brief survey in Appendix A and analyzing your results in Chapter 7, you can determine your negotiating style and explore ways to become more flexible. In addition, certain communication skills such as questioning and listening, or being more direct and assertive, will serve you well in negotiating. You identify not only your present style but also skills to broaden your repertoire of responses and improve your success in negotiating.

- *To select and use tactics conducive to a win-win outcome:* Many books, articles, tapes, and other materials have been published espousing a win-win philosophy. However, most don't provide specific tactics and techniques to achieve such an outcome. As you see in Chapter 8, the specific tactics and behaviors that ensure the best chance for a positive outcome are fully explored.

- *To respond to adversarial situations and difficult people:* Sometimes people play dirty and use adversarial tactics to gain an advantage. Chapter 9 provides a comprehensive treatment of what these tactics look like and how to respond and counter difficult tactics used by the other party. Since each negotiation is different, it is critical to select the most appropriate tactics for a given situation. Chapter 10 offers a systematic method to determine the tenor of the negotiation, whether it is collaborative, neutral, or adversarial.

- *To plan and prepare for real-life negotiations:* Chapter 11 deals with specific situations such as buy and sell, internal negotiations, negotiating with your boss, and team negotiations. All of the previously described skills and knowledge are linked into a simple yet effective planning process throughout the book, encouraging you to apply these concepts to real-life situations. Chapter 12 walks you through an annotated *Negotiation Planning Guide.*

Audience for Practical Negotiating

Throughout this book, we explore three main areas of negotiating:

1. *Personal situations:* Individual consumers with purchases large enough to warrant negotiation as the technology of exchange such as buying a car, house, or property.
2. *Organizational situations:* Managers and employees who perform standard business functions such as creating a budget, making purchases for their company, negotiating for resources in the company, and so on.
3. *Customer situations:* Selling products and services where a long-term relationship is appropriate.

Most readers encounter at least two of these three situations on a regular basis. When considering negotiation, regard it as a process, not a game. In most cases, the issues and relationship are too important to treat the negotiation as a lighthearted interpersonal romp. Working together, we can develop a better way to plan and execute negotiations and reach more win-win outcomes.

Key Points

☞ Conflict is inevitable. Negotiation is a survival skill.
☞ Conflict is a situation where two or more parties have interests or perceptions that differ.
☞ Negotiation is a process of exchange to resolve conflict and reach a mutually beneficial agreement.
☞ Methods for resolving conflict include mediation, arbitration, litigation, and negotiation.

☞ Negotiation is the process of exchange that provides the highest likelihood of satisfying the needs of both parties, while maintaining the relationship.

☞ Conflict exists in many venues (e.g., in organizations or families; with customers).

☞ Power determines the choice of which process of exchange to use (i.e., not engaging, fixed price, bargaining, or negotiating).

SECTION ONE

Planning the Negotiation

CHAPTER

2

Wants and Needs

The best way to get what you want is to help the other side get what they want.

—Ronald Shapiro, *The Power of Nice*

Win-Win Agreements

Identifying and satisfying the underlying *needs* of all parties represents the essence of the negotiation process. Commitment to this outcome creates win-win agreements.

Previous workshop participants have defined a win-win outcome as:

- All parties perceive value in the agreement.
- Mutual agreement that both parties reached/achieved their goals or strategies, and left a window open for change.
- A mutually beneficial agreement achieved between two or more parties that satisfies *all* needs.
- When parties are satisfied that:
  - —Enough objectives have been met such that all sides feel the agreements are fair.
  - —Neither party feels they have lost or that the other party has lost.
  - —The long-term relationship is still healthy and valuable, and has been supported.

A win-win agreement occurs when the underlying needs of both parties are satisfied.

Practical negotiating demands movement and sometimes compromise on your *wants, but not on your needs*. However, many times people fail to distinguish between wants and needs.

Wants versus Needs

When I introduce this concept in workshops, I mention that I cite a number of sources and experts in the field of negotiation, but there is one group who really nailed the concept of wants and needs—Mick Jagger and the Rolling Stones. Usually, this draws a laugh. Then I ask, "What does Mick say about wants and needs?" The participants chorus back the song line: "You can't always get what you want."

"Don't stop there," I say. "What's the rest of it?" Again, most know the next line: "But if you try sometimes you just might find you get what you need." As the first step in the planning process, it is essential for the negotiator to understand this distinction and to work through the possibilities. A colleague of mine uses the following story to illustrate the differences between wants and needs:

> I got up hungry in the middle of the night and had my sights set on those two pieces of leftover pizza in the refrigerator (the want). I also have a teenage son who eats everything in sight, and lo and behold the pizza is *gone*. So, I have to get in touch with my need—hunger. I realize I can't get what I want but, by focusing on the need, I can explore other options such as a sandwich or a bowl of cereal.

Various terms and expressions are used throughout the literature on conflict resolution to describe *wants* and *needs*. Wants correspond to the positions both sides take in the conflict, and needs correspond to their respective underlying interests. There is a direct relationship between the *issues* (i.e., the subjects or topics about which the conflict exists), *wants*, and *needs* in a negotiation.

Negotiators express different wants depending on their perspective on the issue. The difference between wants and needs is illustrated in the award-winning film *Chariots of Fire*.[1] In a classic scene, Eric Liddell, the track star from Scotland, is ushered into a tense meeting of the United Kingdom's Olympic Committee. The conflict arose because Liddell, a Christian, refused to participate in a race scheduled for a Sunday—his Sabbath. As a matter of national

21

TABLE 2.1 Wants versus Needs in *Chariots of Fire*

Parties	Eric Liddell	Committee
Wants	Not to run on Sunday	Run in scheduled event
Needs	Respect Christian Sabbath but still compete	National pride

pride, the Olympic Committee refused to approach the sponsoring nation, France, to request a change in the schedule. During the meeting, both sides restated and defended their wants without looking beyond the issue to the key underlying needs. After a heated exchange, both sides sat silent in a deadlock of wills (see Table 2.1).

Enter Lord Lindsay, another runner on the U.K. team, who breaks the deadlock with a simple suggestion, "Another day, another race." With this new option, all involved realize the elegance of the solution and that they have the power to implement it. (If only we had a Lord Lindsay in every conflict—someone with enough distance from the battle to offer such an option.) Liddell is then substituted for Lindsay in the 400 meters on Thursday, going on to win the gold medal. By running on another day, Eric Liddell satisfies his need to respect the Sabbath. In similar fashion, by arranging a mere change in race participants, the U.K. Olympic Committee did not have to go "hat in hand" to the French to change the event; thus, allowing them to maintain their national pride.

Consider the following analysis of the Camp David negotiations (see Table 2.2):

When Egypt and Israel were negotiating over the Sinai Peninsula in 1978, their positions on where to draw the boundary were completely incompatible. Despite great diplomatic ingenuity during the Camp David talks, no proposed map worked for both sides. Each attempt gave either too much territory to the Egyptians (in the eyes of the Israelis) or to the Israelis (from the Egyptian point of view). How could the two sides get beyond the impasse?

When the negotiators probed beyond their opposing positions, they uncovered a vital difference of underlying interest

TABLE 2.2 Wants versus Needs at Camp David

Parties	Egypt	Israel
Wants	Greater share of Sinai Peninsula	Greater share of Sinai Peninsula
Needs	Security	Sovereignty

and priority: the Israelis cared much more about security, while the Egyptians cared much more about sovereignty. Rather than a simple compromise over where to draw the line in the sand, the value-creating solution was a demilitarized zone under the Egyptian flag.[2]

As we can see from the previous two examples, arguing over positions leads to a series of attack-defend spirals with both parties restating what they want. Only when the parties go beyond positional arguments can they discover the underlying needs and reach a workable solution.

Distinguishing between Wants and Needs in Sales Situations

A common sales negotiation issue is *price*. Buyer and seller want different things. The seller may want a price or rate increase, while the buyer may want a decrease (or for the price to remain constant). The underlying interests are the relevant *needs* of both sides (see Table 2.3). For the seller, the need may be to increase total revenue, while the buyer's need may be to stay within budget guidelines or reduce costs.

Can *both* parties' needs be satisfied? Yes. If the parties explore beneath the surface, they can reach an agreement by working

TABLE 2.3 Wants versus Needs in Sales

Parties	Seller	Buyer
Wants	Price increase	Decrease in price
Needs	Generate additional revenue	Stay on budget and reduce costs

through alternatives. The seller gets additional revenue if the buyer commits to more volume through a longer contract, and the buyer gets to keep the price already budgeted.

Distinguishing between Wants and Needs in Management Situations

Managers in organizations often have a *want* that they believe is the best or the only way to solve a problem. Take the manager whose department is expanding its service offerings to other departments within the company. She wants two new staff people to handle the extra workload. In a meeting with her boss and the director of human resources (HR), she discovers that they do not want to bring in new people. As you can see from Table 2.4, there is definitely a conflict at the *want* level between the two parties.

The negotiation will deadlock if both parties continue to state and defend their wants without getting to the underlying needs. If, however, the parties ask a few key questions, they can discover some latitude in options to meet their *needs*. Some key questions can be found in the following discussion:

> BOSS AND DIRECTOR OF HR: What does getting two new staff do for you?
>
> MANAGER: It allows my department to meet the increased demand.
>
> BOSS AND DIRECTOR OF HR: How does that help the company?
>
> MANAGER: If we provide the additional service through my department, we can keep other departments (my cus-

TABLE 2.4   Wants versus Needs in Staffing and Productivity

Parties	Manager	Boss and the Director of Human Resources
Wants	Two new staff	No new staff
Needs	Provide additional services to meet demand	Maintain corporate headcount and budget

TABLE 2.5 Uncovering the Real Needs of Both Parties

Parties	Manager	Boss and the Director of Human Resources
Wants	Two new staff	No new staff
Needs	Provide additional services to meet demand	Maintain corporate headcount and budget
Options to meet needs	Temporary help	Temporary budget
	Consultants	Fee for service with other departments
	Cross-train present staff	Shift staff resources

tomers) from having to find their own resources outside. The quality and security issues alone are worth the cost.

Exploring other options allows both parties to uncover the real needs of both sides and to reach an agreement *without compromising on their needs* (see Table 2.5).

By asking questions, the boss and director of HR surfaced an underlying concern—security—which could be a key criterion in the decision whether to engage consultants or seek an internal solution. In many instances, what one party wants is just the tip of the iceberg. As we know, most of the iceberg is beneath the water level. Effective questioning brings these issues to the surface and enhances the ultimate solution.

Distinguishing between Wants and Needs in Everyday Situations

Let's examine a practical example most of us have some experience with. Say you have been driving your old car for a number of years. It's costing you money in repairs, and it's just not fun to drive anymore. You are bombarded with new car advertisements on television and start wanting a new car. After focusing on several brands and models, your *want* becomes even clearer, and you start to visit

25

TABLE 2.6 Discovering Options

Wants	Needs	Options
New car	Dependable transportation	Late model used car
		Fix up old car
		Car pool
		Ride bicycle

showrooms and explore the Internet. At this point, it dawns on you that you haven't kept up with new car prices and you experience sticker shock. If you really want the new car, you can probably find a way to finance it. If, however, you dig deeper to explore the real *need*, you may discover some interesting options that were previously unconsidered (see Table 2.6).

If we assume the underlying need is "dependable transportation," there are more options available to meet the *need* than the stated *want* of buying a new car. However, if the need was *status*, the options might be more limited and a new car might be the most viable option to meet this need. Let's look at a more extended example of an internal negotiation.

Case: Loan Processing Crisis
Company: Buckingham Bank
Parties: Director of Information Technology Services
           Director of Loan Processing

General Background

Business has been reasonably good over the past few years at Buckingham Bank. Competition is tough and everyone is under pressure to increase productivity while reducing costs. Two levels of management have been eliminated in the last year, which means that managers and directors are expected to make decisions and resolve conflicts at their level without involving higher authority. The bank's information technology (IT) services group develops and maintains computer programs for the other bank departments. Because of the high degree of security and increased automation, the demands on the IT department have been increasing.

Perspective of the Director of Loan Processing

You are in charge of the loan processing department, a critical part of the consumer and commercial credit business of Buckingham Bank. Your automated processing system for real estate loans is complex and slow by industry standards. The bank has just announced a new product that allows for online mortgage applications. Your volume is expected to double in the next year and the present loan processing system can't handle the volume. In a meeting with your staff, you outlined the specification and changes to the current loan processing computer program. If IT could *modify and expand the current program*, you could process and approve loans much faster. Based on the specifications, a major programming effort would be required to make these modifications. Yesterday, you sent an e-mail to IT with a formal project request and the specifications. The director of IT responded, "IT has a six-month backlog. We'll put you in the queue." Without this programming work, you have a crisis. The increase in loan applications makes your request a top priority that should take precedence over other less critical projects. In the past, you had to go to the senior vice president of operations to get timely support from IT and other service groups, which made you unpopular with other directors. You decide to meet with the IT director.

Perspective of the Director of Information Technology Services

You are head of the IT services department that maintains a data center, develops programs, and provides information services to support the other departments in the bank. Requests for IT services have grown much faster than your budget. In the past year, you have not been able to add staff except for a few college interns, and your programming capacity is stretched to the limit. You have a six-month backlog of projects. You don't like to keep your users waiting so long, but you really don't have much choice other than a "first in, first out" (FIFO) priority system. You have struggled with trying to get a task force of users together to come up with a better priority system, but they always claim to be too busy. However, they try to get preferential treatment by claiming their project is a top priority. To them, everything is a crisis. Even if it were a crisis, you have neither the knowledge nor the wisdom to choose one user over another. You have learned the hard way not to show preference and to adhere to the FIFO policy. Yesterday, the director of loan processing requested an immediate program upgrade that would expand and enhance the mortgage loan processing system. A major reprogramming effort is required. With your current backlog, your response was "We want to help, but you'll have to wait your turn." This director has a reputation for appealing to higher authority and you are determined not to be intimidated.

Meeting with the Parties

Let's listen in on a face-to-face meeting between the parties:

> DIRECTOR OF LOAN PROCESSING: You got my e-mail. So, what I'm asking for is a project to modify and expand the current loan processing program. With all the loans coming my way and the pressure for faster turn-arounds, I don't see any other way.
>
> DIRECTOR OF IT SERVICES: I know you need this now, and it would be good for the bank. But, frankly, I don't have the resources to put on it. There's just no way other than putting your project in the queue. There's a six-month backlog.
>
> DIRECTOR OF LOAN PROCESSING: Six months? That's fine for you, but it doesn't solve my problem. This is a top priority with significant revenue potential. Can't you push some of those other less critical projects aside?
>
> DIRECTOR OF IT SERVICES: And disappoint the other users who've been waiting for their projects to come up? No, I

don't think so! Put yourself in their shoes. Would you want someone jumping to the front of the line?

DIRECTOR OF LOAN PROCESSING: No, I guess I can see your point. But, tell me, why is the backlog so long?

DIRECTOR OF IT SERVICES: I have double the projects I had last year, and yet my budget and headcount stay the same. I get requests for new programs every week, as well as re-programming like yours. My staff is working late nights and weekends just to keep up.

DIRECTOR OF LOAN PROCESSING: Well, as I see it we both have a problem: I need the reprogramming done *now*, and you've got a six-month backlog. Let's think about how we might resolve this and get together tomorrow.

Case Analysis

Let's analyze the case with the wants-needs framework. Think about the pressures on the director of loan processing: increase in volume, potential for more revenue (fees), competitors offering faster processing on loan applications. Then, think of the pressures on the director of IT services: more requests with fewer staff, limited capacity to serve users, exposure to corporate politics. No wonder there's a conflict. To get some hint at how to resolve the conflict, we have to look below the surface of the *wants* to the underlying *needs*, as shown in Table 2.7.

TABLE 2.7 Wants versus Needs in Loan Processing Example

Parties	Director—Loan Processing	Director—Information Technology Services
Wants	Modify and expand current program—need it done now	Six-month backlog—get in line
Needs	Faster loan processing, generate fees, compete	Maintain a fair system for prioritizing projects

By stating and understanding each other's underlying needs, the parties have a fair chance of discovering a solution.

Let's see how the meeting progresses the next day:

DIRECTOR OF LOAN PROCESSING: I've been thinking about your budget and headcount issues. I guess I could go outside for some help with this.

DIRECTOR OF IT SERVICES: You mean hire a consultant? That would really cause me problems. I mean, that makes my department look bad. Besides, they have to get oriented to our systems and they need monitoring. That's not going to give you the speed you need on this.

DIRECTOR OF LOAN PROCESSING: I'm not sure there's any other way.

DIRECTOR OF IT SERVICES: Wait! That gives me an idea. I have two college interns returning to my department next week. They could do the reprogramming as a special assignment.

DIRECTOR OF LOAN PROCESSING: Interns? Are you sure they're up to it? This is a critical project.

DIRECTOR OF IT SERVICES: They're good, really competent. And they have worked with me before and they are really familiar with all the latest technology. Besides, it would be a real challenge for them.

DIRECTOR OF LOAN PROCESSING: Would you be responsible for monitoring their work?

DIRECTOR OF IT SERVICES: Absolutely. As soon as they arrive on site, we'll all meet together to spec it out.

DIRECTOR OF LOAN PROCESSING: Great. If I can do anything to move this along, let me know.

DIRECTOR OF IT SERVICES: You know what would really help me? You could serve as a key member of the user committee I'm trying to form. This project is a good example of when users should be involved in setting priorities. Besides, I could use some help next year during the budget cycle.

DIRECTOR OF LOAN PROCESSING: Okay. If we can get this project started right away, I'll do it.

DIRECTOR OF IT SERVICES: Great! Having your support for IT would be a great boost to our credibility.

DIRECTOR OF LOAN PROCESSING: We've got a deal. Get with my assistant to schedule the meeting next week.

The solution of the college interns meets the underlying needs of both parties. The IT director maintains the integrity of the project assignment system while the director of loan processing gets the reprogramming done in a timely fashion. In addition, the IT director gets the bonus of providing the interns with a mission-critical project, and gains a supportive user during budget time. From the other side, the director of loan processing gets a dedicated team of highly qualified college interns to apply the latest technology to meet his programming needs.

In Chapter 3, I explore both business and personal needs, and how these needs have to be considered in ensuring a win-win solution.

KEY POINTS

☞ Identifying and satisfying the underlying needs of all parties represents the essence of the negotiation process.

☞ A win-win agreement occurs when the underlying needs of both parties are satisfied.

☞ Wants refers to expressed desires or positions each side takes in the conflict.

☞ Needs refers to their respective underlying interests.

☞ If you must, compromise on your wants, but not on your needs.

Practical Application

Think about a current (or potential) negotiation. Ask yourself the following questions to separate wants (position) from needs (interests).

- What do you *want*?

  _____

  _____

  _____

- What would getting this (want) do for you?

  _____

  _____

  _____

- Is this your *need*? If you're not sure, ask the question again: What would getting this do for you?

  _____

  _____

  _____

3

Setting Objectives and Determining Positions

A skillful negotiator will most carefully distinguish between the little and the great objects of his business, and will be as frank and open in the former, as he will be secret and pertinacious in the latter.

—P. Stanhope, 1694–1773

Needs and Objectives

Although identifying your own critical wants and needs is an essential step in the negotiation planning process, it will serve you well to work through what you think *the other side's* wants and needs might be. Ask yourself two questions:

1. What are *you* trying to accomplish in this negotiation?
2. What are *they* trying to accomplish?

Answering these questions leads you to two types of *negotiation objectives:*

1. *Business (or substantive):* Increase revenue, gain market share, reduce costs, acquire a key customer, get resources from another department, buy a decent house at a reasonable price, get a fair property settlement.
2. *Personal:* Enhance a reputation within the industry or community, maintain a strong relationship with the other party, look good to management, increase the individual's power in future negotiations.

Creating a Needs/Objectives Matrix

One way to look at these needs involves a Needs/Objectives Matrix[1] that helps to separate the business from the personal needs in the negotiation (Figure 3.1).

	Your Side	Other Side
Business		
Personal		

FIGURE 3.1 Needs/Objectives Matrix

To create a matrix, list as many needs as you can think of for your side. Then list what you think the needs of the other side will be. Next, circle those that are most critical for you. Then, do the same for the other side.

Some negotiators have a hard time distinguishing between business and personal needs. To test which need is involved, ask this question: If I substitute another person in the negotiation, will the need still exist? If the answer is yes, it's a business (substantive) need rather than a personal need. Skillful negotiators will focus on *both* types of objectives and ask a series of questions to uncover these needs. Inexperienced negotiators will focus only on the business need and fail to engage the personal need in the negotiation.

Needs/Objectives Matrix Example: Loan Processing Crisis

Figure 3.2 shows how a Needs/Objectives Matrix would look if applied to the loan processing case from Chapter 2. In this example, the personal needs are very important to the success of the negotiation.

	Director Loan Processing	Director IT Services
Business	Faster loan processing Generate fees	Maintain a fair system for prioritizing projects Prevent users from going outside for IT services
Personal	Maintain a good relationship with IT manager Avoid being viewed as a "squeaky wheel"	Not be intimidated by this director Build respect within user community

FIGURE 3.2   Needs/Objectives Matrix: Loan Processing Case

To create a win-win outcome, both parties had to go beneath the surface to discover personal needs as well as business needs.

It might be useful at this point to look at the relationship between wants, needs, objectives, and positions as shown in Figure 3.3. We first focus on our *wants*. By exploring what getting these wants would do for us, we discover our *needs*. Once we have defined needs, our next step is to establish our *objectives*—business and personal. Only after having determined our wants, needs, and objectives are we ready to create our positions.

Using this information may help determine your position and settlement range, as we discuss next.

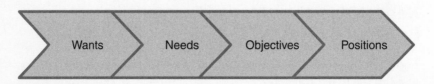

FIGURE 3.3   Relationship of Wants, Needs, Objectives, and Positions

Determining Position and Settlement Range

Position versus Objective

For a specific negotiation, needs and objectives tend to remain relatively constant. If my *objective* is to increase market share or sales volume, this will usually serve as the anchor or focal point for the rest of my plan. Setting objectives ensures that you have other alternatives to getting your needs met (e.g., other clients or sources of supply). These objectives would not change if you moved to a negotiation with another party.

A *position*, by contrast, represents *one way* to accomplish objectives or satisfy needs. Granted, there are probably preferred positions. However, successful negotiators tend to be more creative and flexible about the positions they take. They do not lose sight of the fact that the ultimate goal is to achieve their *objectives*, even if that means that they must alter or modify some of their *positions*.

Settlement Range

Every negotiation involves one or more issues. Successful negotiators plan a *settlement range* of acceptable outcomes for each issue. Less skillful negotiators will go in with just an opening position and any concession or movement from that position feels like a loss. Developing a settlement range is the best insurance against this feeling. The settlement range, generally displayed on a continuum, consists of three main points:

1. *Desired settlement point* (DSP) represents the point on the scale where you believe a "fair deal" can be executed. Ask yourself, "Realistically, where are we likely to settle?" You can look at indices such as market conditions, precedents, comparables, previous deals, and so on. Always set this point *first* in developing your settlement range.

2. *Opening position* (OP) is the point at or above your DSP that you believe meets two criteria: (1) high (but not excessive)

and (2) defensible (i.e., can be argued by using objective criteria or independent sources of information).

3. *Walk-away* (WA) *point* represents the point at which the other party's OP is unacceptable. Determining your WA is a critical part of your planning that prevents you from making a bad deal. Among successful negotiators, there is a saying, "No deal is better than a bad deal!"

In a negotiation for the purchase of a computer, monitor, and printer, the comparative settlement ranges for both the Buyer and Seller are shown in Figure 3.4.

When laid out in this manner, the Buyer and Seller settlement ranges are reversed. In Figure 3.4, the Seller's OP is $1,995 and the Buyer's OP is $1,000—substantially far apart. Fortunately, neither party's OP would cause the other to walk away. Further, we see that the DSP for both Buyer and Seller is about the same—certainly within range. What is the likelihood that this deal will be made? It is very high.

The settlement range represents the operating arena for the computer Buyer if the deal were made with only one currency: cash.

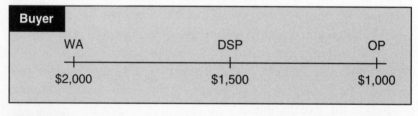

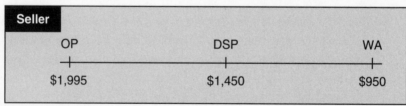

**FIGURE 3.4 Buyer-Seller: Settlement Ranges
(Assume All Specs Are Fixed)**

Buyer and Seller could bargain or haggle over the price or look outside the narrow issue of cash to other currencies. Each party could add significant value to the deal, as shown in the following:

Buyer Offers

- Pay with cash or check to eliminate credit card fee to the seller.
- Purchase maintenance contract.
- Pay for a printer upgrade.
- Purchase additional equipment or software.

Seller Offers

- Maintenance contract at a reduced rate including in-home service.
- Security software.
- Software upgrades.
- Low price guarantee (if buyer finds better price in 30 days, refund the difference).
- Consumables such as printer cartridges.

The offers listed would have a different value for each party, but each could be added to the deal to enhance the overall value.

In Chapter 4, we explore the issue of currencies and how they can add significant value to your negotiations.

KEY POINTS

- ☞ To determine your objectives for a negotiation, ask:
  —What are *you* trying to accomplish in this negotiation?
  —What are *they* trying to accomplish?
- ☞ There are two types of objectives: (1) business (substantive) and (2) personal.
- ☞ Determining *wants* helps explore *needs* leading to *objectives* and *positions*.

39

☞ Effective negotiators develop a settlement range that includes:
  —Desired settlement point.
  —Opening position.
  —Walk-away point.
☞ Using additional currencies can close the gap in the settlement range and enhance the overall value of the deal to both parties.

Practical Application

Figure 3.5 allows you to create a Needs/Objectives Matrix for future negotiations. Consider an upcoming negotiation with a colleague, customer, or any other party. List as many needs as you can think of for yourself, then list what you assume to be the needs for the other side. Next, circle those needs that are most critical for you. Then, do the same for the other side.

	Your Side	Other Side
Business		
Personal		

FIGURE 3.5   Needs/Objectives Matrix: Your Negotiation

Figure 3.6 allows you to create settlement ranges for yourself and your opponent for several issues.

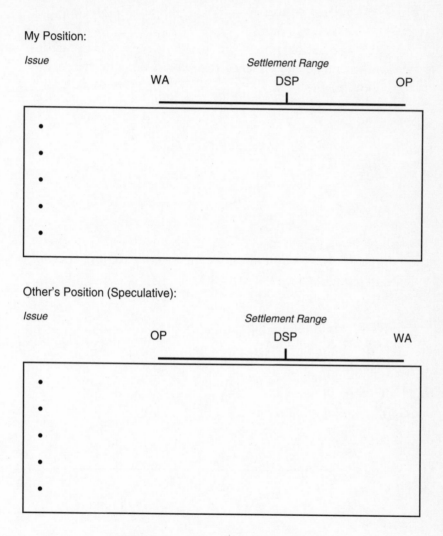

FIGURE 3.6   Position Development

Currencies and Concessions

If you have what the other guy wants, you have a deal.

—Donald Trump

Currencies of Exchange

Because negotiation is a *process of exchange*, the give-and-take of currencies is essential to negotiating. We define *currencies* as tangible or intangible resources that are perceived to have value by the *receiving* party.

Simple transactions involve the exchange of a single currency for a good or service to meet our needs. We exchange currencies every day; in most cases, we do so with the most familiar currency—money. When we broaden the scope from just the single currency to involve other currencies, we are then negotiating.

Currency Exchange in Action

A customer decides to purchase a new refrigerator, finds the one he wants on sale, and is prepared to pay by credit card. The manufacturer's warranty is standard; yet, the salesperson recommends purchasing an extended service plan (ESP) for five years at a cost of 10 percent of the initial purchase price. There is also an icemaker kit for $20, and the delivery and setup costs are $60. With all of these currencies on the table, the customer offers to:

- Pay by cash or check versus credit card (saving the merchant 3 to 6 percent depending on the card).

- Pay for the ESP if the store will send a service tech to his home.
- Get the icemaker kit and delivery/set-up cost for *free*.

The salesperson accepts the proposal and places the order.

Once the other currencies (i.e., cash, ESP, accessories, and delivery) are in play, the parties are negotiating. If both parties are haggling over the price alone, it is bargaining, not negotiating.

Earlier, we discussed how to determine wants and needs. After the underlying needs of both parties have been identified, the next step is to search for and exchange currencies that will satisfy these needs.

When assessing the potential value of a currency, keep in mind that currencies tend to have value in proportion to how well they satisfy the needs of the other party. The best possible outcome is to identify currencies that are perceived to have high value to the receiving party yet are of little or no cost to the providing party. In the example of the refrigerator, the accessories and delivery are a low cost to the store. In similar fashion, the customer could use either cash, check, or a credit card. Because the ESP is a high margin product, once this was agreed to, the store was more amenable to negotiating on the other items.

Types of Currencies

In identifying different currencies, be as creative as possible. As the number of available currencies increases, there is a greater likelihood that a win-win agreement can be reached. Currencies can be divided into three types:

1. *Prime currency:* The central focus of the negotiation, usually money in the form of price, rate, or discounts. In most

instances, the prime currency is the key component of the Opening Position.

2. *Alternative currencies:* Things that one party has that might meet the needs of the other party. Often, alternative currencies can close the gap when two parties are far apart on prime currency. These can take many forms, as we see later.

3. *Elegant currencies:*[1] Things that are of high value to the receiver but that are low cost to the provider.

Creative Currencies Exercise

In negotiation workshops, I have often used an exercise involving the creative use of currencies.[2] Participants are paired up and each contributes $5 to the pot. The rules state that the pot has to go to one or the other participant—no splitting, no giving to charity or a third party, and that the agreements have to be real (deliverable within three weeks of the workshop). Once they know the rules and the identity of the other party, participants are given 10 minutes to plan. They consider two questions:

1. If I *give* the pot, what do I want in return from the other party?

2. If I *get* the pot, what am I willing to give to the other party?

In planning, they have to think about the other party and make some assumptions about what might be valuable to them. They also have to think through their own wants and needs and consider currencies the other party might offer to meet those needs. Participants make lists covering both contingencies—getting or giving the pot. After planning, they negotiate in pairs for 15 minutes and then declare (1) a "deal" and post the results on the flip chart or (2) a deadlock and the money goes to the instructor. Having done this exercise in many different organizations and in public sessions, I am always amazed at the results. Here are just some of the many settlements:

A: Got the pot.
B: Ride to the airport in A's rental car.

B: Got the pot.
A: Day-long sailing trip in San Francisco Bay on B's boat.

A: Got the pot.
B: Job lead in A's division.

B: Got the pot.
A: Help in installing and running new sales tracking software.

A: Got the pot.
B: Recommendations on restaurants and entertainment in A's home city.

After the exercise, I ask participants two questions:

1. Those of you who *gave* the pot, did what you receive have a higher value to you than $5?
2. Those of you who *got* the pot, did what you gave cost you less than $5?

In 90 percent of the cases, the answer to both questions was a resounding "Yes!" This brief exercise heightens the awareness on two fronts. First, we have more currencies than we realize. Second, the value of a currency is in the "eye of the receiver"; in many cases, this can be a true win for both parties. Take the sailing trip, for example. The person who offered the trip had to have a minimum of two people to sail his boat. His wife didn't like to sail that much, so he was constantly looking for passengers to crew with him. What an elegant solution!

Categories of Currencies in Negotiation

Let's push the thinking on currencies even further by suggesting some different categories. Because currencies of exchange are synonymous

47

with resources, they can be tangible (e.g., money, equipment) or intangible (e.g., recognition, time). Here are some examples of currencies:

- *Financial:* Even though money is considered *prime*, there are many ways other than price/rate to directly contribute to the bottom line in a negotiation such as volume discounts, lower rates with a longer term contract, extended payment terms, leasing options, or rent-to-own. When dealing with employees, financial currencies can include salary, bonus, overtime, budget discretion, commissions, tuition reimbursement, vacation time, conferences, or professional meetings.

- *People:* This may include loan of staff, consulting services, your own willingness to participate and work side by side with the other party, dedicated personnel, technical assistance in implementation, administration, or help with regulators.

- *Facilities:* You may own a facility, co-locate equipment, host a test or demonstration site, or agree to serve as a storage facility or parts depot.

- *Equipment:* Equip facilities through purchasing, borrowing in the start-up phase, providing a replacement if equipment can't be repaired in a timely fashion or extra equipment during peak periods.

- *Priorities:* This may include a willingness to accelerate installation, swap a deadline or priority with someone else, or longer term contracts.

- *Information:* This may consist of sharing your expertise, industry knowledge, technical consultation, access to specific data and information, referrals, and serving as a reference.

- *Recognition and rewards:* This may include formal awards, willingness to give credit or acknowledgment, "favored vendor" status, partnering of customer and supplier, joint advertising, praise about an employee given to his or her manager, presenting at professional conferences, or exposure to other industry people.

- *Proprietary agreements:* This may consist of special rights or privileges, first access to new technology, copyrights, geographic exclusives, or "last look" in contract bidding, "right of first refusal."

- *Mitigation of risks:* Parties may need to minimize or eliminate risk (real or perceived by the other party) and discuss price escalators, warranties, guarantees, indemnification for loss, and upgrades to eliminate risk of obsolescence.

The previous list just scratches the surface of possibilities. Karl and Steve Albrecht in *Added Value Negotiating*[3] suggest four questions to identify opportunities to add to the total value equation:

1. What are the elements of value in the deal, both tangible and intangible (i.e., currencies)?
2. What can I give them that they need?
3. What can they give me that I need?
4. How can we both add value to the deal?

By asking these questions, you can expand the list of potential currencies *and* ensure that those currencies are *tied to specific needs—* theirs and yours.

Currencies in Complex Selling Situations

In some customer situations, there may be levels of complexity that provide greater opportunities to offer currencies. If you look at the transaction from the customer's perspective, you might ask:

- How can we make it easier to do business with us?
- How does this customer receive our goods and services?
- What do they do with these after they receive them?
- How do they distribute and sell to *their* customers?

In thinking through these questions, Tom Reilly, in his *Value-Added Selling*[4] series describes at least six types of potential currencies:

1. *Purchasing:* What can I do to help my customer *purchase* and pay for my products or services? An electronics firm, for example, takes credit cards (versus invoice and purchase order numbers) from customers to expedite delivery. Also, some firms use blanket purchase orders.

2. *Inbound logistics:* What can I do to help my customer *receive* my products or services? A parts manufacturer participates in the customer's just-in-time inventory program by establishing a demand-based ordering system.

3. *Operations:* What can I do to help my customer *use* my products or services? A software supplier provides on-site training during the installation and implementation phase.

4. *Outbound logistics:* What can I do to help my customer *distribute* my products or services? A healthcare products distributor provides barcode labels to conform to the drugstore chain's inventory and distribution system.

5. *Marketing and sales:* What can I do to help my customer market and sell using the strengths of my product's features and benefits? A battery supplier provides point-of-purchase displays for stores and coupon flyers for local newspapers.

6. *Service:* What can I do to help my customer maintain and service their equipment? A construction equipment dealer offers "sacrificial customer service," providing a customer parts or a service technician 24/7, every day of the year. It could also include service reminders and product upgrades.

For each of these six areas, think through your customer's business by asking:

- How does this customer incur or measure costs?
- How does this customer measure profit or gain?

At the end of this chapter, an Inventory of Value-Added Currencies (see *Practical Application*) helps you list your offerings by *revenue enhancement* or *cost reduction*. In addition, think about *your business* and how you serve customers. What are some of the special currencies that you could offer to benefit both you and the customer when doing business together?

Concessions

Concessions are a natural part of every negotiation. After all, negotiation is both give and take. What distinguishes successful negotiators is *how*, *when*, and *on what* they make *concessions*—which are defined as giving any or all of a currency.

Key Considerations in Making Concessions

Remember: *Every behavior communicates.* This is especially true with concessions. Because concessions are essential to negotiating, there are some key considerations in planning for and in making concessions:

- *What will the other party infer from my concession?* Will they perceive me as giving in or rolling over? Will they infer that I asked for too much in my opening position and, therefore, I might be willing to make an early concession just to keep them at the table?

- *When should I make a concession?* If I am the first to make a move, will they assume I'm more flexible? Don't make a concession until both opening positions are out. The other party may try to get you to make an early concession by responding harshly to your opening with a statement like, "You've got to be kidding! That's just not acceptable." Instead of conceding anything, ask "What is your position?"

- *How much (or what size) of a concession should I make?* Depending on your planning, you might start with a small concession and see if the other party makes a move. Imagine the signal sent when you make an initial large concession. The other party might believe your opening was far too high, and continue to move for more concessions. If you make smaller and smaller concessions (or stop making them), the other party could perceive that you are at the limit of your concessions and thus might be forced to offer some movement.

- *What is the cost/value ratio of the concession?* What will this concession cost me versus the perceived value to the other party? Do *they* perceive the value of what I'm offering? A common mistake salespeople make in negotiating involves not knowing the true "street value" of what they're offering. Ask yourself the question: What would it cost them (other side) to purchase this separately, or from another supplier? As an example, consider technical support. Most companies have technicians on the staff whose job it is to help customers in the implementation phase. The salesperson may blithely give away this service without realizing the value to the customer. Most companies say that technical support is worth $250 to $500 per hour.

- *What can I receive for making the concession?* Before offering a concession, ask yourself: "If I move on price, are they willing to increase the volume commitment, or extend the length of the contract?" Some currencies are interrelated. Pricing is often tied to volume and length of the contract. One way to look at this is by imagining a triangle (Figure 4.1).

The Currencies Triangle

Let's take a contract with the following parameters:

Price discount = 10 percent
Volume commitment = 10,000 units
Length of contract = Two years

52

FIGURE 4.1 Triangle

As the supplier, you have put together this triangle based on market conditions and current rates. The parameters make good business sense and the deal is profitable. The customer responds that he wants a deeper discount—12 percent. He wants to extend the line by X (see Figure 4.2).

(Note: The inside area of the triangle must remain proportional.)
The supplier can then respond with two options:

1. If you want an extra pricing discount (12 percent), I want a larger volume commitment—say, 15,000 units.

2. If you want an extra pricing discount (12 percent), I want a longer contract—say, three years.

Figure 4.3 shows how the two options look as triangles. Making a concession on the pricing discount allows the supplier to get something of value in return, making this a win-win outcome.

Pricing Discount   + X

FIGURE 4.2 Pricing Discount

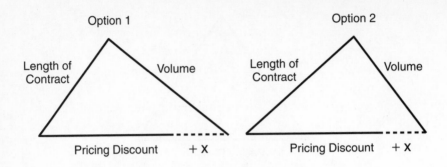

FIGURE 4.3 Triangles for Option 1 and Option 2

Strategies for Making Concessions

In addition to the previous key considerations, other strategies for making concessions include:

- *Always get something in return.* If done for goodwill, acknowledge it. One of the classic errors made by inexperienced negotiators involves giving something to the other side in the interest of maintaining goodwill in the relationship but not labeling the offer. Skillful negotiators will label their concession: "I'm doing this in the interest of goodwill" or "In order to keep things moving, I'm willing to . . ."

- *Look for elegant concessions (i.e., low cost/high value).* Before making a concession, analyze the value of your currencies by assessing the cost to purchase the same item separately. In many cases, service contracts on electronics or other consumer goods can provide a customer with peace of mind while providing a high margin gain for the store. As demonstrated in the creative currencies exercise described earlier in this chapter, the currencies we control may have a much higher value to the other party than we realize. The secret is to analyze the other's needs and make appropriate concessions that are low cost to you, but high value to the other.

- *Agonize where appropriate.* In the enthusiasm to make the deal, salespeople sometimes make the error of offering a concession by saying "Sure we can do that for you." Even though it might be easy to engineer, the best approach is to hesitate and say, "I'm not sure I can do that, let me check to see what [fill-in-the blank with some authority, sales manager, or company policy] says." On the buyer's side, you may really desire the item, but be cautious. If the real estate agent knows you love the house and are already mentally moving your furniture into it, you are likely to find a firmer position on price. A better tactic involves saying: "That would really stretch the budget" or "I'd like to look at other properties to get a better sense of the market."

- *Use your settlement range as maneuvering room.* One of the best reasons to develop a settlement range becomes obvious when we are considering a concession. If you focus on your Desired Settlement Point, you can add or subtract the value of the currencies in play and determine if the deal still meets your needs and expectations.

- *Make the concession and move on.* Timing is important. Unlike agonizing as mentioned earlier, if you have to offer a concession, make it and move on. You do not want the other side to continue to pursue this issue on the table. This is where a partner on your side can be a great asset. Shifting the speaker signals a move to a new issue.

- *Watch your pattern of concessions.* If you progressively increase the size, the other party may try to prolong the negotiation. *How* you make concessions communicates as much as *what* you concede. During the negotiation, be aware of your time limitations. If you have to reach agreement by a certain time, you may feel forced to make concessions earlier in the process than you had intended. When the other side senses that you are under deadline pressure, they may try to delay the negotiation to see if you will make additional concessions.

Making Positive Exchanges

During negotiations, it is important to maintain positive exchanges by using the following techniques:

- *Use "if-then" language.* To maintain balance in the negotiation, don't make a concession without getting something in return. Using the framework of "If . . . , then . . . ," provides a method of signaling the reciprocity that you demand: "If I pay full price, then I expect free delivery." However, be willing to offer something in return for what you want: "If I can get more staff for this project, then I can guarantee that we will meet your deadline." By connecting the two concessions, you are indicating a balance in concessions.

- *If you're stuck, involve the other party.* Offering to do something else to help often breaks a deadlock or introduces more currencies than initially offered. As we see in Chapter 8, brainstorming generates options that may help to break an impasse. A more general way to expand the pie includes involving the other party by saying, "What else could we do that will satisfy both our needs?"

- *Don't give all your currencies or resources to the other party.* After listing some concession options, ask comparison questions: "Which of these is more valuable to you?" If the other party insists on too much, give him a choice: "I can't give you both more equipment and three more support personnel. Which one would you prefer?" A preplanned settlement range for each issue will determine how much you are willing to offer and what value it has to the other party.

- *Signal an expectation for reciprocation.* The concept of *psychological reciprocity* involves the expectation that the other party will give something in return based on your willingness to make a concession. The message is, "In the interest of moving the deal ahead, here's what I am willing to do; and I hope you'll take this in the right spirit and reciprocate." At this point, you can determine whether the other side is willing to move or will dig in even further. Often, skillful negotiators will make a low-cost concession to see whether the other side reciprocates. Information is often exchanged as an early currency. Note whether and how much the other side is willing to share. In many cases, this signals whether the negotiation will be win-win or adversarial. Chapter 10 covers this in detail.

- *Tie the concession to an explicit need.* This is by far the best way to ensure that the other side sees the value of what you are offering. Use the framework: "As I see it, this [concession] will solve [this problem]." By tying your concession to the specific need or problem identified by the other party, you make it difficult for him to say no.

- *Develop your Best Alternative to a Negotiated Agreement (BATNA).*[5] Based on the principle that *no agreement is better than a bad agreement,* your power is increased by having alternative ways to meet your needs. While planning or executing a negotiation, ask yourself: "What alternatives do I have if I can't reach a satisfactory agreement with this party?" As we see in Chapter 5, identifying other alternatives increases your power dramatically.

Key Points

☞ Currencies are tangible or intangible resources that are perceived to have value by the *receiving* party.
☞ Types of currencies:
  —*Prime:* Usually money or the central focus.
  —*Alternative:* Things that one party has that might meet the needs of the other party.
  —*Elegant:* Currencies of high value to the receiver, but with low cost to the provider.
☞ Categories of currencies in negotiations:
  —Financial   —Information
  —People   —Recognition and rewards

    —Facilities   —Proprietary agreements
    —Equipment   —Mitigation of risk
    —Priorities

☞ Currencies in complex selling situations:
    —Purchasing   —Outbound logistics
    —Inbound logistics —Marketing and sales
    —Operations   —Service

☞ Concessions are defined as giving any or all of a currency.

☞ Key considerations in making concessions:
    —What will the other party infer from my concession?
    —When should I make a concession?
    —How much (or what size) of a concession should I make?
    —What is the cost/value ratio of the concession?
    —What can I receive for making the concession?

☞ If currencies are interrelated, consider using a currencies triangle.

☞ Strategies for making concessions:
    —Always get something in return: if done for goodwill, acknowledge it.
    —Look for elegant concessions that are low cost/high value.
    —Agonize where appropriate.
    —Use your settlement range as maneuvering room.
    —Make it and move on—concession timing is important.
    —Watch your pattern of concessions—if you progressively increase the size, the other party may try to prolong the negotiation.

☞ Making positive exchanges:
    —Use "if-then" language.
    —If you're stuck, involve the other party.
    —Don't give all your currencies or resources to the other party.
    —Signal an expectation for reciprocation.
    —Tie the concession to an explicit need.
    —Develop your Best Alternative to a Negotiated Agreement (BATNA).

Practical Application

Currencies/Options

Your Side	Other Side
Considering what you know about their needs, what currencies might you offer to meet those needs?	Considering my needs, what currencies might they offer to meet those needs?
•	•
•	•
•	•
•	•
•	•

Inventory of Value-Added Currencies

Category	Revenue Enhancement	Cost Reduction
Purchasing		
Inbound logistics		
Outbound logistics		
Operations		
Marketing and sales		
Service		

Power in Negotiation

Necessity never made a good bargain.

—Benjamin Franklin

The Paradox of Power

Salespeople lament:

> Power! Are you kidding? Our customers have all the power? How can we negotiate when they're holding all the cards?

Managers complain:

> I really feel like I have no alternative but to work through that department. I mean, they're the people who are supposed to help us, but it's like trying to get blood from a stone!

Purchase agents ponder:

> That vendor is a sole supplier. I feel powerless; as if I have to put up with any price or conditions that they set. They've really got us over a barrel—at least for now!

In numerous seminars with salespeople, managers, and others who have to negotiate for resources, I find an interesting phenomenon. Most people approach a conflict feeling like they are in a less powerful position than the other party. Many conclude that there is nothing they can do to affect the situation. This self-defeating attitude leads to inaction. Both parties are generally interested in reaching a workable agreement, so why do people feel powerless?

Perception of Power

Actual power is difficult to assess, so most of us rely on our perception of power. This perception may be based on a previous experience or our lack of planning. Determining the power balance can affect the manner in which you negotiate. If you feel that the power balance is in your favor, you may not take the time to prepare or foster a good working relationship. If you feel the other side is more powerful, you may become discouraged and again not plan sufficiently to fully explore a win-win scenario. Most of the tactical planning for a negotiation is usually done in a moving vehicle— often in a plane or car on the way to the negotiation. Preparation improves our confidence level and our perception of power. What can you do about real power in a negotiation?

There are many misconceptions about the relationship between power and win-win. One author asserts: "When you destroy the guy across the table, that's negotiating. When you make him thank you for it, that's POWER!"[1] This position represents the direct opposite of my approach. In a true win-win, both parties meet their underlying needs and the relationship is sustained or improved in the process. Thus, *how* you negotiate as well as *what* you negotiate affects the outcome—win-win, win-lose, or lose-lose.

The Rule of Power in Negotiation

Keep in mind one simple rule: In negotiating, power is a function of *alternatives*.

Think of alternatives on three levels:

1. Alternative sources.
2. Alternative currencies.
3. Alternative skills and behaviors.

Because these three levels are cascading, explore alternative sources first. Having exhausted that category, develop any alternative currencies. Finally, consider alternative skills and behaviors that you could use to maximize your power in presenting alternative solutions.

Power in Alternative Sources

In beginning a negotiation, you must first determine your basic needs—not what you *want* but the *need* that must be satisfied. The first mistake in negotiating is to equate needs and wants. For example, you *want* a new car—a Honda Accord. There are a number of dealers who handle this car. There is no sole source, so you can be confident that you do not have to take the first deal. However, think about how many more options you have if you consider your real *need*. If the need is reliable transportation, would fixing your old car be an alternative? How about other models or a used car?

Determining alternative sources of supply is the first step in discovering your power. Even if you are in love with a specific make, model, color, and design, there are other new cars you could select. You might even consider a used car. Is the status quo an option? Do you really "need" a new car? What is the problem that purchasing a new car solves? Reliability? Status? Step back a moment and focus on the real need. The underlying need could be as simple as reliable transportation. When reduced to this elemental term, we can expand the list of alternatives even further—using public transportation, riding a bicycle, roller-blading, car-pooling, or driving a motorcycle. What steps could you take to make the status quo a more viable option?

In a similar fashion, the car dealer has alternatives as well—other customers who might purchase the same car you want. Consider the situation of the Toyota Prius. When Toyota introduced the hybrid Prius in 2001, it represented the only vehicle of its type in that price range. Those who wanted to buy a Prius (at any price) were placed on dealer waiting lists. Toyota was the sole source—high power. This represented a virtual "take-it-or-leave-it" position with dealers charging a premium over the sticker price. Now, with the introduction of similar models, you are in a much better position to negotiate. But, there's still a waiting list.

Salespeople are obsessed with competition and see competitors under every purchaser's desk. They overlook the fact that buyers are usually restricted in their ability to access competitive sources. Among these limitations are:

- Sources located too far away.
- Source that failed to perform and got the purchaser in trouble.
- Preferences of production and engineering people.
- Built-in specification designs that exclude some suppliers.
- Sources that offer a full line of service while others don't.

Uniqueness of a need can lead to a reduction of power because it limits the sources. Consider the high price tag for human organ transplants. Conversely, if a person has a unique solution, their power position increases. Think of the patent holder of the Anthrax vaccine.

In most retail sales situations in the United States, the supplier adopts a "take-it-or-leave-it" position. There's the price clearly marked on the tag. Why? Because retailers have alternatives. Other customers will purchase the products and services they offer. As Herb Cohen says, "Everything is negotiable."[2] But other costs often are more important. If a grocery store negotiated every food purchase, the lines would never clear the registers. Imagine negotiating with a newsvendor for the *Wall Street Journal*:

YOU: I'll give you 50 cents.
VENDOR: No way, the price is 75 cents.
YOU: Okay, how about 60 cents.
VENDOR: Get lost!

Meanwhile, you've just spent over a minute on a transaction that should have taken 10 seconds. If you make $100,000 a year, that conversation cost you about 80 cents and you still had to buy the paper for 75 cents. Was it worth it?

Let's take an example of an internal negotiation:

A distribution manager wants to update the bar code readers in the warehouse to more effectively manage product distribution. In approaching the product managers, she encounters resistance because the new equipment requires a complex changeover, including new labeling and inventory numbers. This is an example of one person's solution becoming another person's problem. What are the distribution manager's alternatives? First, she must identify the underlying need: information to enhance distribution efficiency. The manager should think, "Are there any other ways I could get this information? Perhaps I could use fax or phone to get the information, but that would be time consuming and inefficient and thus is not a viable alternative. Maybe I could find other sources of programming services like other departments, outside vendors, or even a packaged program."

Picture a continuum with one end labeled most viable alternative (MVA) and the other end labeled least viable alternative (LVA), as shown in Figure 5.1. List each option on the continuum.

Certain options may require more resources on your part to ensure a successful outcome; you may have to consider adjusting your expectations. The manager from the previous example may find an outside firm to do the computer programming, but it would take six months to get them up to speed on the current system before they could make the necessary upgrades. Or there may be an organizational ban on using outside consultants when there are internal resources available.

Salespeople, especially in major account situations, find themselves managing one or two customers. With fewer alternative sources available, they really have to rely on creative uses of currencies. In any case, once you have exhausted any viable alternative

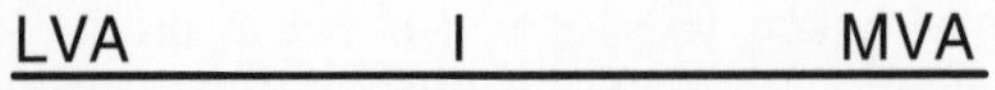

LVA   I   MVA

FIGURE 5.1   Least Viable Alternative versus
Most Viable Alternative

sources for satisfying your need, the next step involves assessing your alternative currencies.

Power in Alternative Currencies

As defined earlier, currencies are tangible or intangible resources that are perceived to have value by the receiving party. When assessing the potential value of a currency, keep in mind that currencies tend to have value in proportion to how well they satisfy the needs of the other party. Liquid currencies of fixed value (i.e., money) can more easily be valued and therefore are considered more powerful. However, if you explore the underlying needs of the other party and discover alternative currencies, there is a much higher chance of reaching a win-win agreement.

As we demonstrated in Chapter 4, the best possible outcome involves identifying elegant currencies—high value to the other party, but low cost to you. Creativity in identifying different currencies is often called "expanding the pie." As the number of available currencies increases, so does your power. Because these alternative currencies appeal to the needs of the other party, there is also an increased likelihood that a win-win agreement can be reached.

Recall that currencies of exchange are synonymous with resources. They can be tangible (e.g., money, equipment) or intangible (e.g., recognition, flexibility), as shown in the following:

- *Financial:* Including salary, bonus, overtime, budget, money.
- *People:* Loaning staff, willingness to participate as a "pair of hands."
- *Facilities:* Using your own facility, hosting a test or demonstration site.
- *Equipment:* Using your own equipment/facility, agreeing to use external sources.
- *Priorities:* Extending a deadline, swapping something or with someone else, agreeing to use some of your own time to contribute.

- *Information:* Providing expertise, industry knowledge, technical consultation, access to specific information and data.

- *Recognition and rewards:* Giving a formal award, credit, or acknowledgment; praising an employee to his or her manager.

- *Proprietary agreements:* Providing first access to new technology, copyrights, or geographic exclusives; "last look" in contract bidding; "right of first refusal."

- *Mitigation of risks:* Minimizing or eliminating risk—real or perceived by the other party.

Salespeople often find themselves locked in a battle over price and regard making a pricing concession as the only way to break a deadlock. In many cases, they miss opportunities to score points with a customer because of "currency myopia." A seller may have premiums or other currencies that are of no additional cost to them or their company. Some may even be beneficial to both parties. An account manager for a telecommunications firm may offer technical consulting to a customer during a negotiation. The telecom company has technical consultants on staff, so there is no additional cost in using them. Although the customer could use the technical assistance, the hidden value may not be obvious. By providing in-depth consultation, the telecom company can gather useful information about the customer's business and use this information in similar business applications. In addition, the customer wins because the on-site help ensures the best technical application for the company.

In negotiation training sessions, participants brainstorm all the possible goods or services they could offer. Next, they review the list and circle those that are elegant—low cost/high value. Do the same with a colleague when planning your negotiation. You will be surprised by the length of the list.

Here's a practical example:

In a real estate transaction, a colleague and his family were relocating and, on their first house-hunting trip, found the perfect suburban home. The price was just out of reach, and the sellers would not reduce it. Instead of giving up, the

68

buyer discovered that his new company would pay for a rental for up to three months until his family could find adequate housing to purchase. So he and the seller agreed to lower the price and added a three-month rental agreement. The buyer paid the price he wanted for the house and the sellers got the difference in price from the revenue of the three-month lease; a true win-win.

Power in Alternative Skills and Behaviors

You can enhance your power in a negotiation by using a variety of skills and behaviors to improve the relationship. Again, *how* you negotiate is as important as *what* you negotiate. A skillful and flexible negotiator can often overcome other power disadvantages. If you can present a proposal or currency in several ways, or in a unique way, you can change the value of that currency in the other's eyes. It is not only having the currency that is important, but also positioning it so that the other side will appreciate and value it. Chapter 11 explores this further in the section on the value proposition.

Positioning a Currency to Show Value

A full-service compensation and benefits consulting firm was negotiating a contract with a large financial services client to revamp their employee benefits plan nationwide. The client balked at one line item with a high price tag— the $50,000 communications package. This item included brochures, videotapes, presentations, and other media to communicate the changes to the employees about the company's new benefits plan. Normally, the consultant would react by defending the price or making a modest concession. However, the consultant took a different approach. By asking the right questions, the consultant discovered that the last time a change like this occurred, the company's human resources staff had to dedicate three months to the effort. By further probing, the consultant discovered that the presentations in the field did not go well and resulted in many unanswered questions. To fully implement the plan, the human resources function had to install a special hotline with a full-time staff person to respond to inquiries. Many employees still resisted the new plan. The consultant then worked up the figures of what this rollout actually cost. The company realized that $50,000 was a bargain for the communications package and accepted the contract.

By refining the tactics involved for when to tell and when to ask, you can increase flexibility and power. Chapter 7 discusses how to increase your skill level.

Power of the Relationship

Without question, developing a good working relationship with the other party can do a great deal to ensure a win-win agreement. Fisher and Ury refer to this as the "power of commitment."[3] We have encountered numerous situations where the best price was not the driving criterion for a successful outcome. In many cases, the strength of the relationship can overcome differences between one deal and another. In all probability, you have purchased things or even hired someone, not because they were the cheapest or the best, but because of a high level of trust between the parties.

Some recommended behaviors to help build relationships include:

- Acknowledging emotions or feelings—yours and theirs.
- Working hard to understand their position, and presenting your own in a way that is understandable.

- Separating understanding from agreement. You can understand *and* disagree.
- Listening to what they're saying *underneath* what they're saying.
- Treating the other side with respect even though you disagree.
- Disclosing selectively to build trust.
- Acknowledging that you recognize the value of and indicating appreciation of any disclosures from the other side.

In negotiation, as with most communication, *every behavior communicates*. Make sure that the message you are sending is what you intended to send.

As you consider an upcoming negotiation, analyze all of your alternative sources, currencies, and skills. In so doing, you increase your power even when the other party seems to hold all the cards.

KEY POINTS

☞ Determining the power balance can affect the manner in which you negotiate.

☞ In negotiation, *power is a function of alternatives*.

☞ Think of alternatives on three levels:
—Alternative sources.
—Alternative currencies.
—Alternative skills and behaviors.

☞ Don't forget the power of the relationship. Develop a good working relationship with the other party to ensure win-win agreements.

Practical Application

Table 5.1 demonstrates the assessment of the power balance in a negotiation.

TABLE 5.1   Power Assessment

Our Side	Their Side
Alternative sources	*Alternative sources*
•	•
•	•
•	•
Alternative currencies	*Alternative currencies*
• Plenty available to close the gap	• Plenty available to close the gap
• Sufficient to close the gap	• Sufficient to close the gap
• Need to generate/explore	• Need to generate/explore
Alternative skills	*Alternative skills*
•	•
•	•
•	•

The following case represents a real-life situation that allows you to apply the planning skills discussed so far in this book. Chapter 12 provides an annotated version of the complete *Planning Guide*, and a blank form is included in Appendix B. In this section, you will have a full practice case including:

- Background information known to both parties.
- Buyer's exclusive information, as represented by the director of telecom for Rough-Rider Outfitters.
- Seller's exclusive information, as represented by the senior account representative for Voice Response, Inc.

Case: Contract Negotiation
Parties: Voice Response, Inc., and Rough-Rider Outfitters

Background Information Known to Both Parties

The seller, Voice Response, Inc., is an entrepreneurial electronics firm that designs and produces voice response systems. These systems sort and route incoming phone calls based on digital selection by the caller. When Voice Response, Inc., started 15 years ago, they were the industry leader. Since that time, other electronics companies have captured market share through a combination of reliable technology and low-cost applications. Voice response technology has come a long way, and customers are demanding the newest and latest system. Clearly, a well-functioning voice response capability is a competitive advantage. This is especially true in the catalog sales business.

The buyer, Rough-Rider Outfitters, is a catalog house specializing in equipment and outerwear for mountain climbers, hikers, and other sports enthusiasts. With a major warehouse and distribution network centered in Boulder, Colorado, Rough-Rider plans to expand its product line and target market this year. They want to add casual sports clothes and accessories and to target young professionals. Rough-Rider's present customer base prefers telephone ordering so that they can discuss the specific features of the equipment before purchasing.

Until this time, Rough-Rider's phone, fax, and website ordering systems were sufficient to handle the 3,000 orders per day. Based on the new marketing initiative and industry projections, orders are expected to increase to an average of 10,000 per day, with peak periods of 15,000. In addition, the marketing department plans to increase the frequency of catalog publication from 4 times per year to 12. Rough-Rider plans to launch their new product line in the winter catalog (six months from now).

Over the past several months, the Voice Response, Inc., senior account representative and the telecommunications director of Rough-Rider have been meeting to work out the specifications for a state-of-the-art voice response system that will permit a customer to place the entire order with a touch-tone phone. Because of the extensive merchandise offerings and various catalog publications, developing system specs has been a monumental task.

The project specifications call for a voice response system that has to be custom designed and installed, with the system configuration for an initial 40 phone lines (ports). The design and production phase is expected to take three months, with installation about one to two weeks. Voice Response, Inc., has proposed using their new Spectrum System.

The negotiation of the contract for the new voice response system is to be completed by the parties today.

Buyer: Rough-Rider Outfitter's Director of Telecommunications' Exclusive Information

Over the past six months, you have been screening voice response vendors for a new marketing venture. By far, Voice Response, Inc., provides the best state-of-the-art technology, but they are not the least expensive. Rough-Rider has been known for its quality equipment and outerwear, but has positioned itself with the serious backpacker and mountain climber. Your customer loyalty has been a landmark in the industry, but the director of marketing wants to expand the customer base. Until this time, your phone, fax, and website ordering systems were sufficient to handle the normal volume of calls per day. The operators were friendly and knew some of the customers personally. Rough-Rider was a nice little business in a great location with serious customers.

You have been working closely with a marketing communications consultant who recommended Voice Response, Inc., as the vendor who could deliver such a complex voice response system. This is your first foray into this technology and you are not totally convinced it will work. Recently, at the annual Telecom Association trade show, you saw some equipment demonstrated, and you were impressed with the capability of voice response.

You suspect that you would be one of the first customers for Voice Response, Inc.'s new Spectrum System. Your main concerns are that the system is user friendly, does not upset your loyal customer base, and is installed on time to support orders from the winter catalog.

In this negotiation, senior management agreed on the following parameters:

- *Contract price:* $200,000 for design and installation of the voice response system based on specifications. (Management has authorized you to go as high as $250,000, if there are other concessions. However, the time schedule must be met; that is, the project must be completed in six months.)

- *Payment terms:* Half of total payment at installation, with the last half paid 30 days after technical sign-off.
- *Software upgrade:* Free software upgrades for three years.
- *Hardware upgrade:* (e.g., 40 to 60 phone ports) at 10 percent to 15 percent of the original system cost (your telecom consultant told you that these costs normally run from 15 percent to 25 percent).
- *Warranty:* Five years.
- *Other issues:* In addition, you would like Voice Response, Inc., to consider:
  —Maintaining absolute secrecy about the marketing program, new technology, and so on until Rough-Rider can announce the new service in its catalogs.
  —Granting exclusive right to the software for a three-year period.
  —Providing on-site technical support during peak periods (Christmas and early spring).

Seller: Voice Response, Inc., Senior Account Representative's Exclusive Information

You have been a senior account representative with Voice Response, Inc., for five years. During that time, you have seen the company lose market share. Most of the business has been lost because engineering over designs systems that exceed customer specifications but that are often delivered late. Other companies in the voice response business have been offering simpler technology but not with the technical sophistication of Voice Response, Inc., systems. Your company has also built a reputation on 24-hour responsiveness to technical trouble.

Your boss, the new vice president of marketing, seems to be just the kind of person to help Voice Response, Inc., regain market share. There is a major advertising campaign underway using the slogan "high technology, top quality, on time." Your boss is anxious to have at least one major system in place to use as a reference and potentially as a demonstrator of Voice Response, Inc.'s technical superiority. Engineering is very excited that their new product Spectrum promises to be the only voice response system of its kind. The Voice Response, Inc., executives are banking on this new product to reestablish them as technology leaders. Rough-Rider is the first large customer to come along with the complex specs that are right for Spectrum.

Over the next two years, Voice Response, Inc., is planning to fine-tune Spectrum and will be developing some very sophisticated software to work on the system. You know that the applications engineers are looking for a test site to put this new software to work.

In this negotiation, senior management agreed on the following parameters:

- *Contract price:* $300,000 for design and installation of the voice response system based on specifications. (Management has authorized you to go as low as $225,000, if you can get the buyer to agree to serve as a demonstration site).

- *Payment terms:* One-third at design initiation, one-third at equipment delivery, and the last third at technical sign-off by the customer.

- *Software upgrade:* Usually free for first year. Subsequent years at 5 percent of the total equipment contract for five years.

- *Hardware upgrade:* (e.g., 40 to 60 phone ports) at 25 percent of the original system cost.

- *Warranty:* Standard is two years, with up to a three-year extension for 5 percent of original contract.

- *Other issues:* In addition, you would like Rough-Rider to consider:
    —Endorsing the new Spectrum System in their catalogs and in trade publication ads.

—Allowing Voice Response, Inc., to use the system as a test station for new software until final testing and installation.

Case Analysis

This case represents a real-life situation. The intention here is to demonstrate how to use the *Planning Guide*. For ease of reading and analysis, we use Seller (Voice Response, Inc.) and Buyer (Rough-Rider Outfitters). In a typical negotiation, you would have more information for your side and less confirmed information about the other side. However, in this case, you have the background information *and* the specific information for each company. After each step, we review what we know. (Keep in mind that this is merely the first part of the *Planning Guide*. Both parts are contained in Chapter 12 and Appendix B.)

Practical Negotiating: Planning Guide—Part 1

Step 1: Determine Wants and Needs

The *wants* and *needs* of both parties are shown in Table 5.2.

Create a Needs/Objectives Matrix

To create a Needs/Objectives Matrix, we distinguish *business* and *personal* objectives, as shown in Table 5.3.

Analysis of Step 1

By laying out the *wants* and *needs* in Table 5.2, we can push beyond the initial statement of wants into the underlying needs. After distinguishing *business* and *personal* objectives in Table 5.3,

TABLE 5.2   Wants and Needs

Seller: Voice Response, Inc.	Buyer: Rough-Rider Outfitters
What do you want? Large customer to install and demonstrate new product—Spectrum.	*What do you want?* State-of-the-art voice response system in six months.
What would getting this (want) do for you? Demonstrate technical superiority. Provide a test site.	*What would getting this (want) do for you?* Improve quality and quantity of customer orders. More transactions, fewer people on phones. Higher profits.
Is this my need? If you're not sure, ask the question again: What would getting this do for you? Increase revenue and market share.	*Is this my need? If you're not sure, ask the question again: What would getting this do for you?* Impress new market segment—young professionals.

we can move into determining position and settlement range. As you can see in the Needs/Objectives Matrix, there are specific issues that may be in conflict. For example, Rough-Rider's need for secrecy versus Voice Response, Inc.'s desire to celebrate their new Spectrum system.

TABLE 5.3   Needs/Objectives Matrix

Needs/ Objectives	Seller: Voice Response, Inc.	Buyer: Rough-Rider Outfitters
Business	Demonstrate the technical superiority of Spectrum. Beta test site for new software. Regain market position.	Install user-friendly voice response system to handle increased volume. Secrecy about new marketing program.
Personal	Please your boss by landing this major deal for Spectrum.	Maintain quality of customer ordering system. Don't upset the present customer base.

Step 2: Position Development

Figure 5.2 shows the Seller's position and settlement range (top). The Buyer's position and settlement range are shown in the bottom chart.

Voice Response, Inc.
Settlement Range

Issues	WA	DSP	OP
• Cost	$200K	$250K	$300K
• Terms	1/3	1/3	1/3
• Software	Free–3 yrs.	Free–2 yrs.	Free–1 yr.
• Hardware	10% of initial cost	15%	25%
upgrade 40–60			
• Warranty	3 yrs.	3 yrs. at 5% of initial cost	2 yrs.

Rough-Rider Outfitters
Settlement Range

Issues	OP	DSP	WA
• Cost	$200K	$225K	$250K
• Time	3.5 months	6 months	6+
• Terms	½ on install and ½ 30 days after final technical sign-off		
• Software	Free–3 yrs.	Free–2 yrs.	Not free
• Hardware	10% of initial cost	15%	15%+
upgrade 40–60			
• Warranty	5 yrs.	3 yrs.	2 yrs.

FIGURE 5.2 **Position and Settlement Ranges for Seller (Top) and Buyer (Bottom)**

Analysis of Step 2

The first thing to observe is the Seller's opening position (OP; $300,000) versus the Buyer's walk-away (WA) point ($250,000). If the Seller holds firm, the Buyer has no choice but to find an alternative to meet their needs. However, if you compare their respective desired settlement points (DSP), they are clearly within range ($25,000) of making a deal. Also, the Seller has no time frame in the settlement range and the need for speed is very important to the Buyer. Settlements of all of the other items are within range.

Step 3: Currencies/Options

Each side must consider their needs and those of the other side. From the Seller's side, based on what they know about the Buyer, they might ask, "What currencies might we offer to meet the Buyer's needs?" The Seller might consider:

- Priority status in system development so that the Buyer can meet their aggressive timetable.
- 24-hour responsiveness to technical problems.
- Technical support during peak periods.
- Network administrator training.

From the Buyer's side, based on what they know about the Seller, they might ask, "What currencies might we offer to meet the Seller's needs? The Buyer might consider:

- Being a reference for other noncompetitive customers.
- Serving as a demonstration site.
- Allowing release of information about the new Spectrum system after the winter catalog is issued.

Analysis of Step 3

In the planning phase, we have just scratched the surface of available currencies. In the dialog that would occur in the actual negotiation session, the parties might uncover a number of currencies and options to meet their needs.

Step 4: Power Assessment

Analysis of Step 4

As we see from Table 5.4 showing a breakdown of alternative sources, neither Buyer nor Seller is at a marked advantage. Voice Response, Inc., could find another company with the sophisticated application needs to warrant their new Spectrum system, but it takes time to develop the application specifications. At the same time, Rough-Rider could add phone lines, operators, and fulfillment staff to handle the increased volume. However, neither of these alternatives looks attractive since they would not meet the underlying needs and objectives of the parties.

TABLE 5.4   Alternatives

Seller: Voice Response, Inc.	Buyer: Rough-Rider Outfitters
Alternative sources	*Alternative sources*
• One other large customer may be interested, but not for three months.	• Other voice response vendors from the trade show have called with additional offers. • Stay with the current system and hire more phone operators and fulfillment staff to handle the increased orders.
Alternative currencies (check one) ☐ Plenty available to close the gap. ☑ Sufficient to close the gap. ☐ Need to generate/explore.	*Alternative currencies (check one)* ☐ Plenty available to close the gap. ☑ Sufficient to close the gap. ☐ Need to generate/explore.
Alternative skills • • •	*Alternative skills* • • •

In Chapter 12, we introduce the complete *Practical Negotiating: Planning Guide*, which takes us through:

- Planning to execute stages.
- Assessing your negotiating style.
- Determining your tactical orientation.
- Tactical selection.

SECTION TWO

Executing the Negotiation

Negotiation Model: Stages with Critical Tasks

Respect your fellow human beings, treat them fairly, disagree with them honestly, explore your thoughts about one another candidly, work together for a common goal and help one another achieve it.

—Bill Bradley

Stages: The Negotiation Process Road Map

Up to this point, we have been working through the planning phase of a negotiation. In this chapter, we are going to explore the process of negotiating—when you are actually engaged with the other party. This simple three-stage model has been presented in hundreds of workshops on negotiation for both sales and management audiences. There are probably other models for the phases of a negotiation, but, because *simplicity ensures applicability*, this model is simple and easy to remember. We use this model as our road map throughout the book to guide us in determining strategy and tactics and to help with planning a team negotiation.

Think about the Negotiation Stages Model (Table 6.1) as both a macro- and micro-level model. Most extended negotiations take place over a series of meetings. On a macro level, you may see the negotiation extend for months with each meeting focused on only one stage or critical task. The parties meet for the opening stage to establish the issues and agenda; then return to their constituents to determine the positions and currencies they might offer at the next meeting. On a micro level, each meeting usually has an opening, exploring, and closing stage.

TABLE 6.1 Negotiation Stages Model

Stages	Critical Tasks
Opening	Set the climate and agenda. Establish the process. State and respond to opening positions.
Exploring	Distinguish between wants and needs. Identify alternative currencies/options. Match currencies to needs.
Closing	Summarize the agreement and contract. Communicate and implement.

Opening Stage

In the opening stage, much of the tenor and tone of the negotiation is established. Climate issues may include:

- *Location:* Will you meet at your place or theirs?
- *Seating arrangements:* Will members sit across table or at each end? Will there be team seating?
- *Access to technology and communication:* Is there a phone, fax, computer, Internet, or calculator?
- *People:* Who is there and who is not?
- *Time frame:* How much time is allocated for this meeting?
- *Refreshments:* Will there be any? If so, what kind?

Set the Climate

In the opening stage, *every behavior communicates.* If the other side intends to have a collaborative, win-win type negotiation, they will work to establish a positive climate. Many unskilled negotiators are so quick to get down to business that they ignore this critical juncture in the process. During the Paris peace talks to end the Vietnam War, there was a climate issue about the "shape of the table." At first, I thought this was a euphemism for shaping the agenda. However, this issue had to do with the literal shape of the negotiating table and the seating arrangements. The parties had to negotiate this issue before any substantive progress could be made. In a negotiation with one of our clients, we arrived on time, but were kept waiting, and later were faced with three additional people at the meeting, one of whom turned out to be very confrontational. Whether they intended to or not, the opposing side's behavior set an adversarial tone.

Many years ago, I worked for a home warranty company training "conciliators" to serve as mediators between home buyers and builders. When buyers pay a large amount for a new house and discover that the roof leaks, the pipes freeze, or the foundation is cracked, they and the builder are not likely to exchange pleasantries at the negotiating table. Nonetheless, one of our attorneys coined the term *cadence of agreement*,[1] meaning he would begin by saying: "It sure is a beautiful day"; or "What a lovely neighborhood!" Once the adversaries started to agree on something, the resolution of issues was more likely to go smoothly.

Consider the signals we are sending to customers when we negotiate. Do we intentionally work to put them at ease or at a disadvantage? If we are not acting with intention, we may be sending the wrong or mixed signals to the other party. This becomes increasingly important in international negotiations where business protocols are strange or unknown. Many Americans negotiating in different cultures ignore the significance of building a relationship as part of setting a positive climate.

Set the Agenda

In setting the agenda, we again have an opportunity to send a message. Should you set the agenda and get a response from the other party, or vice versa? Giving the other side initial control of the agenda can work in your favor provided you trust they will give you the chance to add or modify. You might respond:

> You mentioned in your e-mail that we plan to deal with X, Y, and Z today. Is that correct? Are there any other issues we need to consider? What about A and B?

Before you actually put your opening position on the table, you can list the agenda items without committing to a value. You might say:

> We need to talk about price, volume, length of the contract, shipping, delivery, and indemnification. Oh yes, and credit terms. Is there anything I left out?

If you have a standard contract or agreement, it may contain all of these items. If not, brainstorm with your negotiation partner before the meeting to see if you can think through all the issues that are likely to arise. Depending on the level of trust, both parties may want to ensure that there are no surprises at the end of the negotiation. Some issues that might be overlooked are contingencies for late deliveries or missed deadlines, indemnification for loss during shipment, liability, and renewal of the contract. In one case, two parties with a long-term relationship had a dispute about whether a contract was "evergreen" (automatically renewable). After a prolonged negotiation and a deadlock, the parties ended up in litigation.

Establish the Process

How are we going to operate in this negotiation? Single meeting versus multiple meetings? What's the time frame? Who are the key players on each team? Who will speak to which issues? The importance of establishing the process should not be underestimated as pointed out by Bordone and Todd:

> *Negotiating the right process for your negotiation is well worth the time and effort for two important reasons. First, process drives substance. Decisions about who is invited to the table, how issues will be discussed and linked to form value-creating trades, and how to make and extract commitments will have a tremendous effect on the negotiation's outcome. Negotiating process options and choices before discussing substantive issues is therefore central to crafting deals that last. Second, a fair process increases legitimacy and satisfaction. A*

person's perception of the fairness of the process used in a negotiation influences not only satisfaction with the substantive outcome but also the willingness to abide by it.[2]

One of the most delicate issues involves *decision-making authority*. In many organizations, there are folks on the front-line who can say "No," but who can't give an unqualified "Yes." Testing this authority can be tough especially if you haven't thought through your approach. Here are a few questions to consider:

(Bad) Are you the decision maker in this deal?

(Better) Once we've reached agreement, what happens?

(Best) How are decisions like this made around here?

Imagine going through the entire negotiation and hearing the words: "This sounds great to me, let me run it by the committee (or my boss)." In some cases, like international treaties and agreements, there is built-in ratification by governmental agencies. Make sure you know the depth of the other's authority.

Other issues in establishing the process could include the use of rules. Some examples include break or caucus time; access to telephones, fax, or Internet; and who can join the negotiation once in progress. Unless you have a compelling reason to institute a rule, don't. Also, be aware when the other side insists on a rule. What are they trying to communicate? What signal does it send when you introduce a new person or procedure into the negotiation?

State and Respond to Opening Positions

Stating your opening position can be a difficult task for people who have not planned or thought through what they really want and need. Opening positions should be verbalized in a forceful but respectful manner. The skills required involve assertiveness—willingness to state your position without qualifiers—as in the following examples:

I need this by next Thursday.

I'm willing to pay $50,000 today.

I want joint custody.

Clear and concise is the key. When you waffle, you signal to the other party that you are not sure of yourself and that you might make an immediate concession if pushed. To develop a comfort level with your opening position, say it three times, looking someone straight in the eye. If you can't say it to a colleague, chances are you won't pull it off when confronted with an adversary.

How high should your position be? In Chapter 3, we discussed how to develop your settlement range. Remember that your position should be *high but defensible*. Can you defend your position using facts, logic, precedents, market conditions, or other objective criteria?

Should you open first? There are two advantages to opening first if: (1) you have planned your strategy and can defend your position if tested; and (2) you are dealing with an unskilled or unprepared negotiator who will adjust his or her position to yours—opening at 10 percent to 20 percent up or down from your opening.

In responding to the position of the other side, first realize that it is a *position*, not the final or even expected settlement point. Make sure you've heard the position clearly. What is the other side trying to communicate in their position? This tactic tends to set the bar and can signal a firm position.

Test the other side's position with questions including:

Are you saying that you want 100 percent of my business, and no less?

As I understand it, that's the extent of your budget? There are no more funds available?

Are there any conditions under which you would extend the deadline?

91

Skillfully used, testing questions can determine the firmness or flexibility of the other side's position.

Work within your settlement range. When the other side's position is below (or above) your walk-away point, you should be prepared to do just that. In workshops, I always ask, "How many of you have ever walked away during a negotiation?" In an experienced crowd, almost all of the hands go up. "Now, put your hand down if that was the end of the negotiation." Amazingly, 80 to 90 percent of the hands stay up. Salespeople in particular find this tactic difficult to execute because they feel they have to stay at the table. Once the other side realizes this, you have lost some leverage in the negotiation.

A negotiation doesn't truly begin until both *opening positions* are on the table. Once you've got the positions out and you've responded to the other party, it's time to start *exploring*.

Exploring Stage

Distinguish between Wants and Needs

In the *exploring* stage, distinguishing between wants and needs is critical. When you have two negotiators who realize that an opening position is just *that*—a place to start—you can begin in earnest to discover the needs and objectives of the other party. With an inexperienced negotiator on the other side, you may find this tough sledding. Often, naive negotiators will want to stay with opening positions and engage in an attack-defend spiral. Skilled negotiators will move beyond this and move into exploring. You can actually feel a change in the energy in the room when someone switches into exploring as illustrated by the following dialogue between a supplier and a warehouse manager:

> WAREHOUSE MANAGER: I want a minimum of 10,000 units in each shipment.
> SUPPLIER: Tell me why that's so important to you.
> WAREHOUSE MANAGER: Well, our warehouse dock schedule is rather tight so we need to handle one or two large shipments rather than several smaller loads.

Once we've identified the *need* (i.e., warehouse accommodation) compared to the *want* (i.e., minimum of 10,000 units), we can explore the skills of questioning and listening and how to use them in the key task: *distinguishing wants and needs*. This is where your planning pays off. If you've done your *needs/objectives matrix*, you can ask lots of questions to test your assumptions.

Identify Alternative Currencies/Options

Once you have a better sense of what is underneath the surface, you can begin to explore and brainstorm alternative ways to meet the needs of the other party.

Using Questioning and Listening to Explore Needs and Identify Options

---

A construction equipment manufacturing company has to raise prices with a long-term customer, a heavy equipment dealership. The dialogue begins with the manufacturer's representative telling the parts manager about the increase:

> MANUFACTURER'S REP: I'm afraid I have some bad news. We have to raise our prices on parts by 10 percent.
>
> PARTS MANAGER: What! I thought we had a deal through the end of the year on all of your parts.
>
> MANUFACTURER'S REP: Yes, I thought we could honor that price as well, but we've been hit hard by steel prices and one of our key parts manufacturers is in real financial trouble.
>
> PARTS MANAGER: But, we're one of your best dealers. How can you do this to us?

93

MANUFACTURER'S REP: I know that this must have an impact on both you and your construction customers.

PARTS MANAGER: It sure will.

MANUFACTURER'S REP: What could our company do to help you with your customers?

PARTS MANAGER: Well, for starters you could wait until next year to raise prices.

MANUFACTURER'S REP: If only that were possible, it would be great. Let's think about it and toss around some alternatives. It seems to me you have a fairly good handle on your customers' peak seasons, you know, when the equipment is in heavy use and parts are in demand.

PARTS MANAGER: Yeah, the spring and summer are peak seasons for all our customers.

MANUFACTURER'S REP: Since we can anticipate the volume you'll need for those periods, why don't we look at the 5 percent volume discount program. Would that help?

PARTS MANAGER: Actually, we could do that. But, I have a better idea. We still have some money in this year's budget for parts. If we did an advance payment as well as advanced ordering, could you give us a better break on the price?

PARTS MANAGER: Let me see what my management can do for us on that issue.

The manufacturer's representative did not back down or make a concession on price, but recognized the difficult position of the parts manager. Exploring alternatives requires disclosure and trust from both parties. Sharing the reasons you have taken your initial position will serve to break the ice. The use of questions to explore the underlying needs led to creative alternatives.

During the exploring stage, you and the other party are offering currencies to try to satisfy the underlying needs of both parties. Picture a flip chart with lots of options and ideas written on it. This is the time to take those alternatives and see what needs they would fulfill. Let's continue the previous discussion:

> PARTS MANAGER: So you're offering a 5 percent discount if I order parts in volume. And maybe we can do better than that if we pay for them in advance. Is that right?
>
> MANUFACTURER'S REP: Yes. I think I can make a strong case for an additional discount if you can order now for next year. Is that possible?
>
> PARTS MANAGER: Well, that could be a problem. You know how small my warehouse is, especially for those big attachments we handle.
>
> MANUFACTURER'S REP: If you order those types of parts, I can store them in our warehouse and drop ship right to your customer's site provided we have the payment in advance.
>
> PARTS MANAGER: Sounds good! Let me go over the volume figures with you.

Match Currencies to Needs

The task of matching currencies to needs involves really understanding what is behind each need and then offering the best alternative or option available. In addition, unless you have great recall, taking notes would be a good practice in *exploring* so that you can refer back to the needs.

Let's continue our look at the earlier negotiation between the Supplier and the Warehouse Manager:

> SUPPLIER: So, if we keep shipments to a minimum of 10,000 that makes it easier for you to schedule the loading crew?

WAREHOUSE MANAGER: Yeah, and if you can give us 48 hours notice, we'll make sure the whole crew is there when the truck arrives and your driver can keep his delivery schedule.

SUPPLIER: Sounds like that would work really well for both of us.

Closing Stage

Summarize the Agreement and Contract

Whether a formal contract or simple handshake, this is the capstone of an agreement. Often, in the blush of optimism, the parties rush through this task—big mistake. The old saying, "If it's not written down, it doesn't exist" applies here. The best technique in this phase is to take the time to go back through each of the items on the agenda to make sure each has been covered. Once both parties can describe and are satisfied with the terms and conditions of the agreement, it's time to wrap it up.

Communicate and Implement

Once the agreement has been signed or made final, it's appropriate to communicate it to the parties who are affected by the outcome. In some instances, the extent of communication is dictated by public interest. However, sometimes the parties insist that the agreement be "sealed," including penalties for disclosure. In any case, how the agreement will be shared with a wider constituency should be discussed and agreed to by the parties.

When an agreement is complex and involves multiple resources to implement, communication become increasingly important. In addition, both parties should explore implementation pitfalls. These usually begin with "What would happen if . . .?" Some examples follow:

What would happen if we don't meet the volume target?

What happens if the car breaks down within the next six months?

How do we handle a delay in the installation schedule?

Granted, you can't anticipate everything, but it is a good idea to spin a few "what if's?"

That's the Negotiation Stages Model with critical tasks. There are other more complex models for the phases of a negotiation; however, if you subscribe to the notion that simplicity ensures applicability, this three-stage model should be easy to remember and follow. The Negotiation Stages Model also works very well in planning a team negotiation, as we'll see in Chapter 11.

KEY POINTS

☞ The model provides an easy-to-follow road map for a negotiation.

☞ *Opening stage:*
—Set the climate and agenda.
—Establish the process.
—State and respond to opening positions.

☞ *Exploring stage:*
—Distinguish between wants and needs.
—Identify alternative currencies or options.
—Match currencies to needs.

☞ *Closing stage:*
—Summarize the agreement and contract.
—Communicate and implement.

Practical Application

Table 6.2 would be useful for taking notes while planning for or executing the stages in a negotiation.

TABLE 6.2

Stages	Critical Tasks
Opening	Set the climate and agenda.
	Establish the process.
	State and respond to opening positions.
Notes:	
Exploring	Distinguish between wants and needs.
	Identify alternative currencies/options.
	Match currencies to needs.
Notes:	
Closing	Summarize the agreement and contract.
	Communicate and implement.
Notes:	

CHAPTER

7

Negotiation Styles and Key Skills

I would not waste my time in friction when it could be turned into momentum.

—Frances Willard (Educator)

The Difference between Negotiation Styles and Skills

Earlier, we stated that negotiation is a survival skill. In that case, how can we identify our negotiating style and build the key skills necessary to respond to conflict when it arises? In a general sense, we all have a natural interpersonal style that affects how we interact with people in a wide variety of situations. You may have been introduced to models of interpersonal and interactive skills in workshops or reading. Here, I plan to build a model for understanding the dynamics of people in conflict where negotiation is the appropriate response.

Negotiation style refers to the general approach or behavioral style you use in negotiating—confrontational, conciliatory, collaborative, and accommodating. In Appendix A, you can complete the *Negotiation Style Survey* that will give you a sense of your negotiating style. By taking the survey, you can also identify key skills to help you adjust your negotiating style, meet your objectives, and sustain relationships.

Key skills are the ability to be assertive and persuasive (i.e., not aggressive and confrontational) and use questioning and listening. These skills will enhance your effectiveness in negotiating—whether you are setting ground rules, presenting your opening position, or exploring underlying needs—and are essential to success. In many ways, these skills are the fundamental communication techniques (similar to reading and writing, or passing and shooting) for executing all of the tactics we explore later in this book.

Choosing the Best Overall Approach

In addition to your negotiating style, there is also the issue of choosing the best approach, or the overall behavior that you select in the negotiation.

Later, we explore specific tactics that support your overall approach. The model in Figure 7.1[1] illustrates how to analyze a negotiation situation based on the importance of (1) the issue and (2) the relationship.

To help interpret the model in Figure 7.1, assume that in a given negotiation, the issue is important, yet the relationship is not of high importance. The appropriate stance in that case is *"take it or*

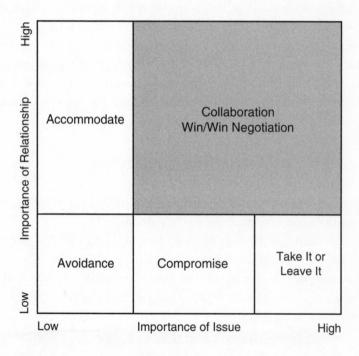

FIGURE 7.1   **Importance of Issue versus Relationship**

leave it." An example of this might be purchasing a car where the relationship with the salesperson or even the dealership is not important. You might take a hard line on price to see how far you can push. In similar fashion, if the relationship is important, yet the issue is not, then it is appropriate to *accommodate*. In a divorce settlement, the issue of where the parties meet may not be important to your side, so, to ensure an amicable process, the other side is accommodated and they select the meeting place. The shaded box of Figure 7.1 (Collaboration—Win-Win Negotiation) represents the area where both issues and relationships are important. The other aspect that I like is the *avoidance* of the topic when neither the issue nor the relationship is important.

When I present this model to salespeople, they often say, "The relationship is always important!" I respond, "Absolutely. But do you need to work on building the relationship *in this negotiation?"* If you have built a solid relationship with this customer throughout the sales process, it may be appropriate around certain issues to take a firm line; for example, when you have to insist on a price increase. If you have a strong relationship, it will probably not be damaged. Often, I will ask them how they negotiate with their spouse. If they really care about an issue, will this threaten the solid relationship they have built? Probably not.

Negotiation Styles

Before we explore the Negotiation Style Model, be sure you have taken the *Negotiation Style Survey* in Appendix A.

The building of our Negotiation Style Model[2] begins with basic psychology and the primal responses to conflict. Generally, people respond by displaying the classic extremes of *fight or flight*. In Figure 7.2, we see these two responses laid out on a continuum.

Fight  Flight

FIGURE 7.2 Fight-Flight Continuum

Focusing on conflict expressed in verbal conversations, here are the characteristics of fight versus flight:

Characteristics of Fight	*Characteristics of Flight*
Loud	Quiet
Forceful	Reticent
Demanding	Accommodating
Aggressive	Passive
Confronting	Avoiding

In responding to conflict, neither of these extremes works well. The fight response focuses on *me*—my needs, position, and so on. By pounding on my position and my issues, the relationship is often damaged. However, the flight response abandons the issues in service of saving the relationship or avoiding the pain of confrontation.

Imagine the dialogues that would occur if two parties were operating at the two extremes (see Figure 7.3).

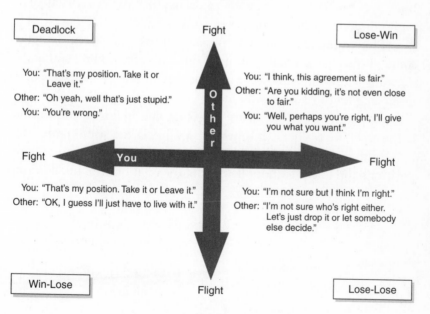

FIGURE 7.3 Fight-Flight Dialogue

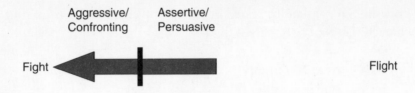

FIGURE 7.4   Fight (Options)

As shown in Figure 7.3, fight-fight usually results in a heated argument, with neither party coming out ahead, and ends in a deadlock—a no-win situation for both. Fight-flight (or vice versa) may get grudging acceptance, but may result in passive-aggressive behavior during implementation. When both parties try to avoid in flight-flight, they either sweep the conflict under the rug or try to get someone else to decide. Neither of the extremes works well. What's the alternative?

Imagine keeping some of the positive characteristics of fight but reining it in a bit. Let's go back to the continuum. Instead of going all the way into behaving with aggressive/confronting actions, we stop half way and use an assertive/persuasive style, appealing to directness and the power of facts and logic (see Figure 7.4).

Picture the same on the other side of the continuum. Imagine some of the characteristics of flight but without avoiding and withdrawing. Here the behavior would be one of openness/responsiveness (see Figure 7.5).

By putting these two figures together, and adding the dimension of the other, we can build a model with a win-win zone (see Figure 7.6).

In the win-win zone, both parties are direct and forceful about positions and issues without damaging the relationship. In addition,

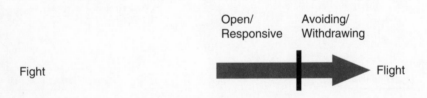

FIGURE 7.5   Flight (Options)

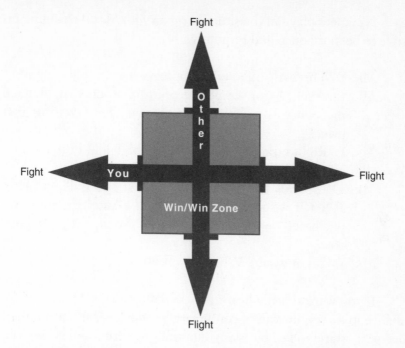

FIGURE 7.6 **Fight-Flight and the Win-Win Zone**

they are more likely to be open and responsive to the other party when there are differences to be expressed. Realistically there are times when one of the parties will cross the line into less productive fight-or-flight behavior. But by using an assertive/persuasive style, combined with the open/responsive style, the other person can draw him back into the win-win zone. The following example of a win-lose dialog might be helpful:

MR. Y: That's my offer, take it or leave it.

MR. O: Oh Yeah! Well, that's way out of line with the current market. That's just ridiculous!

MR. Y: Well, I know the market better than you and I say that's what the traffic will bear. So, I'm sticking to it.

MR. O: I really wanted to do business with you, but you're just too far out of line.

105

Now, let's play out the situation again with Mr. O changing his style to be more open and responsive:

MR. Y: That's my offer, take it or leave it.

MR. O: Well, I can see you're pretty firm on that. But tell me, what is so important to you about getting that price?

MR. Y: Right now, my cost-of-good is high and I can't absorb all of the increased expense!

MR. O: Sounds like we're both against the wall on price. What if we include a clause that adjusts the price we pay based on market conditions? Would that help your cost?

MR. Y: Yes, it would. What do you suggest as a formula?

If you were actually hearing these dialogue, you might sense a change in *energy*; instead of continuing to *push* against one another, one party starts to *pull* by asking questions to better understand the underlying issues. Table 7.1 provides some examples of push and pull behaviors.

What's important here is that neither type of behavior alone is sufficient to successfully carry out a negotiation. Some people have a natural tendency to be push negotiators while others feel more com-

TABLE 7.1   Push and Pull Behaviors

Push Behaviors	Pull Behaviors
Stating your position.	Asking questions.
Holding firm.	Listening.
Persuading logically using	Summarizing.
• Facts.	Being open and responsive.
• Logic.	Acknowledging common ground
• Objective sources.	and areas of agreement.
Asserting.	Seeking to understand.
Offering currencies.	
Seeking to be understood.	

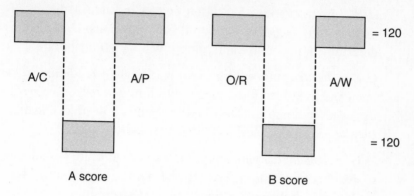

FIGURE 7.7 **Push and Pull Behaviors**

fortable in a pull mode. As you will discover from the survey results, you probably have both capabilities, but a preference for one type of energy. Here's where your survey results come in. If you've done the survey, post your results here. If not, what are you waiting for?

Survey Says?

Figure 7.7 provides a form to record your *Negotiation Style Survey* results.

Analysis

Use the following information to assist in the analysis of your survey:

$$A/C + A/P = \underline{\hspace{1cm}} \text{A Score}$$
$$O/R + A/W = \underline{\hspace{1cm}} \text{B Score}$$

If your A score is significantly higher (20+ points), you tend toward a push style (Aggressive/Assertive). If your B score is significantly higher (20+ points), you tend toward a pull style (Collaborative/Passive).

A/C = Aggressive/confronting: High scores indicate a strong need to control situations and/or people. Described as persistent, tough-minded, dominating, decisive.

A/P = Assertive/persuasive: High scores indicate a direct approach using facts and logic to defend positions. Described as determined, persuasive and logical, willing to collaborate.

O/R = Open/responsive: High scores indicate a tendency to be open and listen carefully, to ask questions and respond regarding needs and issues. Described as open and flexible, conciliatory, approachable, seeking to understand.

A/W = Avoiding/withdrawing: High scores indicate a tendency to avoid confrontation, even to the point of withdrawal. Described as risk averse, cautious, and compromising.

Can I Change My Negotiating Style?

Yes! Your negotiating style is based on your overall behavior pattern in dealing with conflict. Behavior can change with conscious effort, by learning or enhancing the key skills that affect your negotiating style. Let's look at a couple of examples:

Negotiator X

20	55	35	10	= 120
A/C	A/P	O/R	A/W	

Interpretation: Negotiator X has an A score of 75 (A/C + A/P) and a B score of 45 (O/R + A/W). The 30-point difference indicates a strong tendency to push, or an aggressive/assertive style. By looking at the column score, we realize that Negotiator X tends to use an assertive/persuasive approach (A/P) more often than an aggressive/confronting approach (A/C). Even though Negotiator X is clearly a push-oriented negotiator, she tends to rely on a less confrontational approach and would likely not damage the relationship permanently.

However, if Negotiator X negotiates alone—without a partner to balance her push style—she might benefit from developing the key pull skills of questioning and listening.

Negotiator Y

5	45	53	17	$= 120$
A/C	A/P	O/R	A/W	

Interpretation: Negotiator Y has an A score of 50 (A/C + A/P) and a B score of 70 (O/R + A/W). The 20-point difference indicates a tendency to pull or a collaborative/passive style. By looking at the column score, we realize that Negotiator Y tends to use an open/responsive approach (O/R) more often than an avoiding/withdrawing approach (A/W). Even though Negotiator Y is clearly a pull-oriented negotiator, he tends to rely on a more open and responsive approach; therefore, less likely to give in or withdraw. However, if Negotiator Y negotiates alone—without a partner to balance his pull style—he might benefit from developing the key push skills of asserting and persuading.

Negotiator Z

15	47	49	9	$= 120$
A/C	A/P	O/R	A/W	

Interpretation: Negotiator Z has an A score of 62 (A/C + A/P) and a B score of 58 (O/R + A/W). The minor point difference indicates balanced push and pull styles. By having balanced A and B scores and a relatively small number of points at the extremes, Negotiator Z demonstrates the skills necessary to both push and pull appropriately when the need arises. This negotiation style pattern is quite conducive to a person negotiating solo.

Key Skills

You can tell whether a man is clever by his answers.
You can tell whether a man is wise by his questions.

—Naguib Mahfouz

What can you do to develop the skills to change your negotiating style? There are two areas of key skills (1) push skills (i.e., asserting/persuading) and (2) pull skills (i.e., questioning/listening).

Go back to your survey results and see what they reveal about your preference for either push or pull negotiating. Remember, if your A score and B score are 20+ points apart, this indicates a clear preference, and developing the opposing key skills may round out your negotiating style.

Push Skills: Asserting/Persuading

There are many books and workshops on how to be more assertive. The key to being assertive was described simply in three steps by David Berlew[3] as:

1. Know what you want!
2. Ask for it directly!
3. Be willing to pay for it!

As we saw in Chapter 2, distinguishing between wants and needs is essential to your success and satisfaction as a negotiator. Step 1 (Know what you want) involves being very clear about your *want*. Step 2 (Ask for it directly) involves the skills of asserting/persuading, which we cover later. Step 3 (Be willing to pay for it) requires the use of currencies that we covered in Chapter 4. When using this three-step process, I recommend thinking through each step before verbally stating what you want, and then waiting for a reaction. In many cases, when you express what you want in clear terms, the other side may be willing to provide it without the additional incentive of a currency. However, if there is some push-back, you can discover what currency you could offer and gauge the price tag for this request. Then, you can offer the appropriate amount or type of currency.

Approaching a Peer-Level Manager for the Loan of a Key Technical Person for a Day

Dialogue 1

MGR. A: I need Joan (technical person) for a full day sometime in the next week for an important project.

MGR. B: Anytime over the next week? How about Friday?

MGR. A: Great. I'll send over the project report so she knows what's going on.

Dialogue 2

MGR. A: I need Joan (technical person) for a full day sometime in the next week for an important project.

MGR. B: Anytime over the next week? That's not possible! I have Joan working on a critical project with a deadline in two weeks. Sorry, I can't help you.

MGR. A: So, what you're saying is Joan will be tied up for at least two weeks.

MGR. B: Yes. With everything we have going right now, I can't see loaning you Joan for even a day.

MGR. A: So, Joan is out of the question. Is there anyone else in your department that would be available?

MGR. B: Afraid not.

MGR. A: Tell me more about the projects you have Joan working on right now.

111

Mgr. B: Well, she's leading a team putting together a key presentation for the board meeting a week from Thursday. They're struggling with getting the formatting in PowerPoint. You know how the CEO likes all of the slides perfect.

Mgr. A: If I sent my PowerPoint guru over to your department to train your staff would that help free up some of Joan's time?

Mgr. B: Absolutely. Let's do it!

Improve Your Asserting/Persuading Skills

State Your Position or Demands Clearly and Concisely

When you are clear about your position, the other party understands specifically what you are asking. Many of us feel uncomfortable asking for something directly, especially if we do not have authority over the other person. However, think about your own experience and how refreshing it is when someone approaches you directly with what they need rather than tentatively approaching the subject. Courtesy does *not* weaken your position. Consider the following options:

(Bad) Can I ask a favor? If it's not too much trouble, can you possibly do this report today?

(Good) Can you do this report today?

(Better) I need this report today, please.

Provide Solid Facts, Evidence, Proof, Rationale, or Reasons for Your Position

To get what you want, you may have to do some research and provide some reasons for your position. The most important consideration involves framing your arguments based on the other person's template of important facts. Some people respond well to facts and figures, while others want to know the impact on people. Frame your logical arguments for the specific audience across the table, as in the following:

(Good) This report is really important.

(Better) This report is critical to help the board decide on the strategy. The information you generate will clearly lay out the options and provide the facts they need to make recommendations.

Use a Few Strong Reasons—Avoid Argument Dilution

You can sink your boat by providing too much information. Using too many reasons invites the other person to take issue with the weakest reason for your position. Focus on a few compelling reasons rather than overwhelming the other person with more reasons than necessary. The old adage "When the boat hits the shore, stop rowing" comes to mind. The following provides a contrasting example:

(Good) Here are the six reasons why this report is so important.

(Better) This report is critical to our department's budget discussion.

Discovering the limits of logic will help you become a better negotiator. Incentives that address the question, "What's in it for me?" work much more effectively.

Don't Be Tentative—Avoid Using Qualifiers

As we saw in the example on page 112 about being clear and direct, using qualifiers may make you feel less demanding but may water down the forcefulness of your request. Again, distinguish between courtesy and qualifiers—for example, "If you don't mind," is a qualifier; "please" is not.

Don't Become Angry or Emotional—Disengage Instead

As we will see in Chapter 9, your opponent may try to rattle or make you angry—at which point logical reasoning becomes impossible. A much better strategy involves being prepared to disengage or take a break rather than continuing beyond your boiling point. The following statements illustrate different ways to disengage:

I'd like to step back and think about this for a while. How about if we sleep on it and get back together tomorrow?

Things are getting hot. How about taking a coffee break?

Make Concessions Only on a Quid Pro Quo Basis—Get Something in Return

In looking at concession behavior in Chapter 4, we addressed the issue of reciprocity. Getting something in return for a concession helps you to maintain the sense of balance in the negotiation. Being clear, direct, and assertive helps you draw boundaries and signals where you are firm and where you might give a little, as in the following:

> We really cannot go any further without some give from your side. If you were willing to drop your price, then we would agree to make a higher volume commitment.

Be Willing to Offer Something in Return for What You Want

Having made your position clear, the last step is to be willing to pay for it. Just as you expected the other side to offer a currency if you made a concession, you must be willing to offer something to get what you want, as in the following example:

> We want to hold our price at X to send a signal to the market. As I recall, you mentioned that cash flow was a problem for you. How about if we extended the payment terms from 30 to 60 days? We would hold to the price we set and the better terms would help you manage cash flow. Would that do it?

Use If-Then Language

Using an if-then framework (e.g., "If we do X, then you give us Y.") ties together a concession and a request for a currency from the other side. Without this linkage, you might find yourself making a unilateral concession and getting nothing in return.

Pull Skills: Questioning and Listening

As we saw in Chapter 2, making the distinction between wants and needs can accelerate the negotiation process. In their book *Getting to Yes*,[4] Fisher and Ury pointed out that arguing over positions tends to result in unwise agreements, is inefficient, and endangers the ongoing relationship. They showed that there is a better way to negotiate by satisfying both sides' interests and needs. This means that learning how to assess the other side's needs accurately is a critical skill. This is where your pull skills can help you with questioning and listening.

Techniques for Assessing Needs

Ask Open-Ended Questions to Distinguish between Wants and Needs

After listening to the other party's position, ask them "Why?" An even better question is "What does getting that do for you?" This mother-of-all-questions can help you get beneath the surface to the real reason for the other's position. Ask "Why not?" to try to understand the other party's reason for refusing to accept your position. Use "who, what, when, where, and how" questions as well to ensure that you completely understand his or her wants and needs.

Summarize and Paraphrase to Express Understanding

As the opening positions are stated and the exploring begins, step back and summarize. "As I understand it, you're saying that a two-year contract is necessary to lock in this rate. Did I get that right?" Another technique involves *arbitrary mirroring* or stating back in no uncertain terms the firmness of the other's position. "So, you're saying there are no conditions under which you would accept less than full price?"

Use Silence Effectively to Encourage the Other Party to Open Up

In interpersonal communications, most of us are uncomfortable with silence. The old adage "The first one who speaks, loses" may seem glib, but test it yourself. In your next conversation, let 5 seconds to 10 seconds go by and see what happens. Silence can stimulate the other party to make a concession or reveal more about his or her position.

Listen with Empathy to the Other Person

Put yourself in the other party's shoes. Analyze each issue and their position and ask yourself "What is the emotional content here?" Have they been frustrated by the lack of speed? Do they feel pushed by upper management to make this deal? As a skillful negotiator, you can build bridges of understanding with statements of empathy. "It sounds like that was very frustrating." Use empathy to acknowledge areas of agreement: "I'm sensing we both feel the need to come away with a deal that our _____ [clients, spouse, manager] will approve."

Ask Follow-Up Questions

Once you ask a question and listen to the answer, follow up with a question to dig deeper. "So, the discount helps you pass along savings to your customers. What are some other ways you can add value to your customers?" Sometimes we want to go back to an issue that was raised previously but not explored. "Earlier you mentioned, payment terms. Tell me more about how that might help with your cash flow."

Ask "What If?" and "What Else?"

Take the initiative to suggest some options. "What if we provided extra trucks during peak periods? Would that help you meet the tight delivery schedule?" When you have to say "No," add "What else?" For example, "Since we can't provide on-going training after the initial installation, what else could we do to make sure your operators can run the machines safely?" Encourage the other side to brainstorm and together think of alternatives. "Just for a moment, let's step back and throw out some ideas about how to close this gap."

Disclose and Encourage Psychological Reciprocity

To increase the likelihood that the agreement will satisfy your needs, disclose your interests and concerns. Disclosure is a powerful tactic. If you share information about your underlying needs, you increase the likelihood that the other person will reciprocate and share his or her underlying needs or concerns. You set up an expectation that the other side can follow. If they don't, that's a signal.

As you review the results of the *Negotiation Style Survey*, ask yourself: What are my strengths as a negotiator? What are my weaknesses? What can I do to address these? Building the key skills outside your comfort zone helps you modify your negotiation style and become a more versatile negotiator.

KEY POINTS

☞ *Negotiation style* refers to the general approach or behavioral style you use in negotiating.

☞ *Key skills* are those that enhance your effectiveness in negotiating.

☞ In choosing the best overall approach to a conflict, consider the importance of both the issue and the relationship.

☞ The primal response to conflict is fight or flight—neither of which is effective.

☞ By avoiding the extremes of fight and flight, we discover some positive characteristics that help create our negotiation style.

☞ Negotiation style is a combination of four types of behavioral responses:
—Aggressive/Confronting
—Assertive/Persuasive
—Open/Responsive
—Avoiding/Withdrawing

☞ Using the energy of push and pull, we can further discover different aspects of our negotiating style and its effectiveness.

☞ We can change our negotiating style by learning or enhancing the key skills that affect our style.
—Push skills: Asserting and persuading
—Pull skills: Questioning and listening

Practical Application

Use Table 7.2 during your next negotiation.

TABLE 7.2   Negotiating Styles

Your Side	Other Side
Names:	*Names:*
•	•
•	•
•	•
Negotiating style (check those that apply):	*Negotiating style* (check those that apply):
☐ Aggressive/Confronting	☐ Aggressive/Confronting
☐ Assertive/Persuasive	☐ Assertive/Persuasive
☐ Open/Responsive	☐ Open/Responsive
☐ Avoiding/Withdrawing	☐ Avoiding/Withdrawing

Win-Win Tactics

Basically, there are two kinds of negotiations. The first is adversarial negotiations, where one side wins and the other side loses. The other is collaborative "win-win" negotiations, where both sides concentrate on solving the problem in a way that is acceptable to everyone.

—Robert F. Guder

Tactics Defined

Tactics are behaviors—actions used by the negotiator to serve a purpose or to pursue an objective. Tactics can be verbal or non-verbal. As we pointed out earlier, the first rule in communication is that *every behavior communicates*. Whether we want it to or not, our behavior speaks louder than the words or tone we use. Have you ever developed a series of assumptions about a person just by watching him enter a room and shaking hands—even before he utters a single word? Prior to a negotiation, we make assumptions about the other person based on how easy it was to set up the meeting—his tone on the telephone; his receptivity and openness with information before the actual face-to-face meeting.

Tactics can work to strengthen the relationship or to intimidate, discourage, or even anger the other party. Tactics can be skillfully planned or allowed to just happen in the course of a negotiation. The tactics employed to strengthen the relationship and to ensure a win-win outcome are referred to in this book as *win-win tactics*, while those tactics chosen to intimidate or tip the power balance are called *adversarial tactics*. In this chapter, we describe win-win tactics. In Chapter 9, we address adversarial tactics and countertactics as well. There are some tactics that are clearly adversarial or win-win, while others are neutral or depend on the intention of the negotiator. For example, the Agenda tactic can be used to help both parties get their needs met or to produce a one-sided negotiation.

Win-Win Tactics

Win-win tactics, if used by you or the other side, are more likely to lead to a mutually beneficial agreement. Many of these tactics are also referred as "cooperative tactics" for use in "Principled Negotiations."[1] Some of these tactics, if used in a manipulative or extreme way, could result in a negative outcome. Win-win tactics are not intended to be used in this manner. We encourage you to learn how and when to use these tactics. In Chapter 10, we explore a method to determine which tactics to use and which to expect from the other side.

The tactics are listed alphabetically and laid out in the following format:

- *Description:* What the tactic is about.
- *Sounds like:* The words or phrases negotiators use to execute the tactic.
- *Advantages:* Positive reasons to use this tactic.
- *Disadvantages:* How the tactic may backfire or limit your effectiveness.
- *Tips:* General information about the use of this tactic.

Each of the following tactics will allow you to build a win-win outcome.

Agenda

- *Description:* Listing the issues to be discussed in the negotiation.

- *Sounds like:* "We plan to deal with _____ today. Is that correct?" "Are there any other areas we should cover?"
- *Advantages:* Helps you take the initiative and maintain control. Guards against surprises as you work to close the agreement. If you control the agenda, you control what will or will not be addressed.
- *Disadvantages:* May be perceived as too pushy.
- *Tips:* Control of the agenda signals firmness. Let the other side set it to demonstrate flexibility. Always ask for additions or clarifications. In sales situations, make sure that all of the issues are listed, including product or service, price, delivery, service after sale, and so on.

Authority Limits

- *Description:* Establishing the authority or range of decision-making power that you and the other side possess.
- *Sounds like:* "How is this decision going to be made?" "Once we've reached agreement, what happens?"
- *Advantages:* Acknowledges limits up front. Can offer you an out if needed. Identifies gatekeepers and stakeholders.
- *Disadvantages:* Tests the level of trust and credibility early.
- *Tips:* Ask the other side to describe their authority as clearly as possible. What limits exist? Who else might have to get involved? If they do, how long will it take for approval? Additional players or stakeholders may surface in the negotiation. It is best for both sides to determine early in the negotiation who will be involved rather than be surprised at the end (see *Authority Escalation* in Chapter 9). Often, the person you deal with may serve as an initial screen for bids or vendors. A common mistake is to assume this person has no authority and try to go around him. He may not be able to say "Yes," but he can say "No." Make him an ally: "If you were in my shoes, how would you approach _____ [the real decision maker]?"

Balancing the Scales

- *Description:* Displaying or laying out the agreement as if on a scale or ledger so that both parties can compare what they are giving and receiving in the negotiation.
- *Sounds like:* "So, you get a better discount for a larger order, and I get faster payment terms to help me with cash flow."
- *Advantages:* Compares currencies exchanged side by side to demonstrate a fair deal.
- *Disadvantages:* Can show imbalance between the two sides leading to additional concessions.
- *Tips:* Most people will settle for a fair deal especially if they can see it laid out side by side. In many cases, the party negotiating with you may have to demonstrate to someone else that they got a fair deal.

Brainstorming

- *Description:* All negotiators agreeing that for a fixed time (say 5 minutes) they will generate some ideas on how to reach agreement, while at the same time suspending judgment or insisting on a concrete resolution.
- *Sounds like:* "Let's step back and try a few what-if's." "We seem to be stuck here, what if we discuss some options and see if something emerges that we can both live with."
- *Advantages:* Generates lots of options and alternatives without commitment. Signals openness and flexibility to the other side.
- *Disadvantages:* Less control of the process. You may reveal more than you intend.
- *Tips:* Although this could be used early in the negotiation, it is most appropriate during the exploring stage. It is very useful if an impasse has occurred. Establish the ground rules before you start brainstorming.

Bundling

- *Description:* Combining (bundling) currencies to demonstrate additional value (see also the *Currencies Triangle* in Chapter 4).
- *Sounds like:* "If we put together price, volume, and the terms of the agreement, you can see that they all work together to provide you with price stability and a deep discount." "We'll include both technical assistance and on-site service to ensure that your operation doesn't go down."
- *Advantages:* Establishes the added value of two or three items. Demonstrates the interrelationship of currencies such as price, volume, and term of contract.
- *Disadvantages:* Other party may cherry-pick one currency in the bundle while misunderstanding the impact on other parts of the deal.
- *Tips:* Look over your list of issues and see which could be related—price and volume, parts and labor, technical assistance and service delivery, and so on. Using the triangle concept provides you with room to maneuver while maintaining a sense of balance in the deal.

Caucus

- *Description:* Taking a break or calling a time-out during the negotiation, usually to consult with your negotiating team mate or another interested party.
- *Sounds like:* "Why don't we take a break?" "We need a few minutes to . . ." "Let me review your offer with (management, spouse, etc.)."
- *Advantages:* Changes the pace. Prevents bad or one-sided concessions. Helps deal with surprises.
- *Disadvantages:* May cause anxiety if either side is time pressured. Can be perceived as delaying.
- *Tips:* Successful negotiators take breaks more often than average negotiators. Caucuses allow you to review what you

learned, explore possible alternatives, review and modify your strategy and tactics, discuss possible concessions, regain control of your emotions, and consult with others. This tactic is especially useful in team negotiations. You can even call a caucus if you are by yourself.

Change of Pace

- *Description:* Varying your negotiating style—shifting from asserting to asking questions. Speeding up the pace of the dialogue, or slowing it down.

- *Sounds like:* "We need to reexamine some of the earlier points." "We seem to be moving pretty fast here, let's slow down a bit. Now, did you say . . ." "What do you say we wrap this up today?"

- *Advantages:* Keeps you from being too predictable. Creates mild time pressure.

- *Disadvantages:* May be confusing to and misinterpreted by the other side.

- *Tips:* When the other side uses an emotional outburst or a dirty trick, you can maintain control by disengaging rather than confronting. If they are not moving fast enough for you, quicken the pace by asking targeted questions or making short statements. If you regularly negotiate with the same party, periodically change your negotiating style.

Change the Negotiator

- *Description:* Literally, taking yourself or a teammate out of the negotiation or adding a member to the team. Similar to a relief pitcher, this can change the pace and neutralize an advantage that the other side may hold.

- *Sounds like:* "These issues require some technical savvy. Let me bring in _____ [team mate, or expert]." "These new clauses require consideration by _____ [legal, upper management, etc.]."

- *Advantages:* Can break an impasse. Useful to save face or soften a confrontational situation. If you risk a deadlock, consider using it.
- *Disadvantages:* Could create delays or be seen as a weakness.
- *Tips:* The tactic usually favors the one who proposed the change (if you planned on doing it all along). If the other side does it to you, don't repeat the old arguments. Change your position only if they change theirs; call a caucus.

Closing the Deal

- *Description:* Moving the negotiation along when the other side seems reluctant to finally make a deal.
- *Sounds like:* "We seem to have all of the issues covered. What do you say we wrap this up today?" "If not now, when?" "What else do you need to close this deal today?" "So, if we did X, Y, and Z, would you give us a contract today?"
- *Advantages:* Nudges the negotiation to closure. May surface additional issues.
- *Disadvantages:* May appear to be aggressive, if not done positively.
- *Tips:* Trust your gut if you sense reluctance. Make repeated requests for action in a straightforward manner. Ask what's on their mind or making them uncomfortable about the deal. Make closing the deal a real and desirable experience for the person.

Columbo (a.k.a. Playing Dumb) . . .

- *Description:* Patterned after Peter Falk's Lieutenant Columbo who draws out important information by feigning ignorance.
- *Sounds like:* "Could you explain that to me again? I don't think I quite get it."
- *Advantages:* Buys you time to think. The other side may modify their position.

- *Disadvantages:* Other side may view it as initial acceptance of their position.
- *Tips:* Very useful in dealing with an outrageous position. It is less pushy than countering with an equally outrageous position, and the other side may modify their position or take a less arbitrary stand. Reduces confrontation and gains you valuable information.

Common Interests

- *Description:* Acknowledging common concerns or beliefs. Celebrate previous deals that have been a true win-win for both of you.
- *Sounds like:* "We both stand to gain by working together." "We've resolved a lot of issues already."
- *Advantages:* Creates a positive climate. Maintains progress.
- *Disadvantages:* Must be genuine or will be perceived as manipulative.
- *Tips:* Especially in the early stage of a negotiation, describe the mutual benefits of working together. When the issues are likely to be adversarial, use this tactic to acknowledge where agreement does exist. Often, if the other side believes you value the same things, you may find common ground that allows both sides to take another look at concessions. Anytime the negotiation breaks down, review the common ground you have already established.

Concessions

- *Description:* Giving up some or all of a currency to the other party.
- *Sounds like:* "I would be willing to do this_____ , if you would be willing to do _____ ."
- *Advantages:* Can break an impasse. Keeps things moving.
- *Disadvantages:* Has to be done carefully. May be perceived as weakness.

- *Tips:* Always get a concession in return. It's okay to say "No." Use psychological reciprocity: a give on your part coupled with a take. Successful negotiators tend to make consistently smaller concessions, be less generous, and be unpredictable.

Convert the Associates

- *Description:* Influencing a receptive member of the other side to act as an ally.
- *Sounds like:* "Let's meet for a few minutes afterward." "I have some information that might interest you." "How about if our IT specialist talks with your IT person?"
- *Advantages:* Can break an impasse. Useful to save face or soften a confrontation situation.
- *Disadvantages:* Can be perceived as Divide and Conquer (an adversarial tactic).
- *Tips:* If the main negotiator is playing hardball or is difficult to convince, try to use others in their organization to influence the negotiator. Rarely do decision makers operate in a vacuum. Position yourself as providing useful information through informal chats or phone calls. In an internal negotiation, it might be useful to ask for help from a colleague in another department to discover how they influence the person with whom you are negotiating.

Create Empathy

- *Description:* Acknowledging that you understand the emotional tone of what's happening.
- *Sounds like:* "I understand your concerns, and will try to . . ." "Your account is very important to me." "I can see how that issue would affect you."
- *Advantages:* Builds the relationship. People respond to people.
- *Disadvantages:* May unintentionally send the signal that you need them more than they need you.

- *Tips:* Although this could be used early in the negotiation, it is most appropriate during the exploring stage. Never negotiate only in the name of your company; instead, negotiate for yourself as a human representative of your organization. Ultimately, a negotiation is between two people trying to resolve differences. People respond to people. They may not do things for your company; but, they will do things for *you*. Appropriate personal disclosure can do wonders in building a relationship. You can often take a hard position on an issue if you have established a positive relationship beforehand.

Disclosure

- *Description:* Revealing a piece of information or an underlying issue.
- *Sounds like:* "Here's what's really going on in our organization." "Quite frankly, we don't want to loose you. You're a significant customer for us."
- *Advantages:* Builds trust. Can be reciprocal. Often breaks an impasse.
- *Disadvantages:* May reveal too much. May be perceived as weakness.
- *Tips:* If you take the initiative to disclose some information, the other party will often reciprocate in kind. If they are reluctant to reveal more information about their needs, wants, and perceived value of various currencies, it makes it more difficult to find alternative options. Keep in mind that information is a powerful currency, so use it wisely and test the other party's reaction. Do they disclose anything? What do they do with the information you give them?

Expand the Pie

- *Description:* Looking beyond the initial issues to broaden the frame.
- *Sounds like:* "Instead of focusing on your present business volume, how about considering what would happen with

129

25 percent growth next year." "What if we included all the plants in this deal? What would that do for you?"

- *Advantages:* Can break an impasse by expanding the issues. Sometimes, you can get a breakthrough using this tactic.
- *Disadvantages:* Requires trust and participation from the other side. Can focus on issues outside the initial agenda or scope of the deal.
- *Tips:* Think about *all* of the needs for you and the other side. Push your thinking to include issues that would come up in the implementation phase. When buying a car or large appliance, add becoming a reference or referral source to help sweeten the deal.

Face-Saving Techniques

- *Description:* Letting the other party out of something they said that is either unintentionally or purposely untrue.
- *Sounds like:* "I can see how you might have been given old information." "You know I'm not sure I heard you correctly." "Perhaps there are other reasons I'm (or you're) not aware of." "I can understand your proposal on the basis of your assumptions but have you considered . . ."
- *Advantages:* Avoids a personal attack on the other side. Maintains positive climate.
- *Disadvantages:* May appear tentative or unsure.
- *Tips:* People who lose face will take extreme positions: they will suffer losses themselves if it causes their attacker to suffer. Keep your emotions under control, and try not to attack the other person. If possible, blame other third parties or policy.

Mark Up the Document

- *Description:* Literally, making changes to the contract or document and initialing the changes.
- *Sounds like:* "Why don't we change that right here on the contract and initial it."

- *Advantages:* Saves time. By both initialing, you get mutual commitment.
- *Disadvantages:* May be done quickly to get you to make a significant concession.
- *Tips:* Useful especially in contract negotiations. Even the "standard" contract can be changed. As you make changes, initial each and ask for a photocopy of the agreement *before* redrafting. This is often done in real estate or property negotiations.

Objective Criteria

- *Description:* Using facts, figures, or data from an objective source.
- *Sounds like:* "Let's look at some comparable deals." "According to the current published market price . . ." "Standard shipping costs are . . ." "The *Blue Book* value is . . ."
- *Advantages:* Provides credibility to your position. Balances the power.
- *Disadvantages:* Might not agree on "objective" criteria or standards.
- *Tips:* If the other party has more power, structure the negotiation around facts, figures, and accepted precedent. Using objective criteria also helps defuse tension—people don't have to argue with emotions or egos and can justify their decision on neutral grounds. Use comparable products or services to establish and defend your position.

Off-the-Record Discussions

- *Description:* Stepping back and having a side conversation with one of the representatives of the other party—usually your main contact.
- *Sounds like:* "Can we step out into the hall; I have something I need to ask you." "Off the record, is there any way your management would go for this?" "I'm having a

hard time convincing your CFO. Can you help me out here?"

- *Advantages:* Allows for side conversations in private/secret that can get through an impasse or help deal with a difficult person.
- *Disadvantages:* May be perceived as Divide and Conquer. The other side may later deny agreeing to anything said in a side conversation.
- *Tips:* This works well when you are at an impasse or one member of the other party is playing hardball.

Patience/Persistence

- *Description:* Maintaining your cool and focusing on the key issues. Waiting it out, not being pushed.
- *Sounds like:* Often nonverbal. "That's very interesting, let me think about that."
- *Advantages:* Communicates power. Can be very disarming.
- *Disadvantages:* Can be seen as delaying if time pressure exists.
- *Tips:* Patience is often called the *supertactic.*[2] because it can have such a great effect. If time is on your side, you can wait for conditions or the other side to change. Persistence involves sticking to the issues and positions that are most important to meeting your underlying needs and not budging until these needs are met (see also *Soak Time*).

Pinch Factor

- *Description:* Checking with the other party during implementation to ensure that they still feel good about the deal.
- *Sounds like:* "I know that the market has changed. Can you agree to an extension under the same terms?"
- *Advantages:* Maintains relationship by proactively seeking a "good fit" after the deal is done. Shows you really are concerned about their needs and want a win-win outcome.

- *Disadvantages:* If you reopen the negotiation, the other side may want to change other issues.
- *Tips:* Even with a signed contract, the negotiation is not over. If you are truly interested in reaching and preserving a win-win agreement, it is important that you communicate periodically with the other party to gauge how they feel about the agreement. With long-term agreements, it is highly likely that something will change, either internally or externally, and affect the perceptions of one or both parties about how good the deal is. It is better to take the initiative to reopen the negotiation when either side perceives minor discomfort with the agreement, known as a *pinch*, before it turns into outright *pain*. In the latter case, the likelihood of the other side honoring the agreement declines.

Saying No

- *Description:* Simply saying an unqualified "No!"
- *Sounds like:* "No!" "Under these circumstances, there is no way we can meet your demands."
- *Advantages:* Puts a solid stake in the ground. Signals firmness and resolve.
- *Disadvantages:* May cause a walk-away for either side. Must be willing to execute it.
- *Tips:* This can be your most powerful tool in responding to an unreasonable position or demand for a concession. Although it communicates power and resolve, the disadvantage is that you have to be willing to execute it. Remember that it is a tactic and, like a position, it may have to change. Salespeople particularly have difficulty here. They feel they can't say no to a customer. But if the other party knows they are being unreasonable, it can be a way for the salesperson to gain respect. No deal is better than a bad deal that will end up costing your company money.

Scaling

- *Description:* Asking a person to quantify the importance of an issue.
- *Sounds like:* "On a scale of 1 to 10, how important is this issue to you?" "Relative to the other issues, where does this stand in terms of priority for you?"
- *Advantages:* Gives you a perspective on the importance of the issue. Often smokes out side issues or red herrings (an adversarial tactic).
- *Disadvantages:* The other side may not be willing to prioritize their needs.
- *Tips:* Useful when you encounter multiple issues that seem important to the other side, but you need a sense of priority to respond. Helpful when the other side makes an unreasonable demand.

Side Memos

- *Description:* Isolating an issue that either party may not want included in the final contract but that they still want documented. Similar to the Off-the-Record tactic.
- *Sounds like:* "Let's agree to this and I'll send you a separate letter on it."
- *Advantages:* Prevents misunderstandings later. Allows side deals if necessary to ensure the agreement will be acceptable to others.
- *Disadvantages:* Contract policy may preclude the use of this tactic.
- *Tips:* Don't rely on just a word and handshake if the issue is important; the other party may forget or change their mind. Create a side memo that describes the issue and agreement. Have both parties sign or initial it.

Soak Time

- *Description:* Allowing the other party (or you) to think about your offer.

- *Sounds like:* "How about if you think about it overnight and get back to me." "I'm going to need some time to consider this and work the numbers."
- *Advantages:* Acceptance time can break a deadlock. Like a caucus, it gives the parties time to absorb the other's position or offer.
- *Disadvantages:* May be perceived as stalling. Allows the other side to check other sources or their Best Alternative to a Negotiated Agreement (BATNA).
- *Tips:* The idea of soak time is so simple it is often overlooked. Buyers may need time to accept the price increase and to calculate the impact. Salespeople may not be ready to concede on price and may need more facts to make a case.

Summarizing

- *Description:* Specifying exactly what you agreed to at the end of a negotiating session.
- *Sounds like:* "Let's recap the points we've agreed to." "I've written down the agreement. Let's go over it together to make sure I've captured everything."
- *Advantages:* Prevents misunderstandings or omissions. Indicates progress.
- *Disadvantages:* Can be overused.
- *Tips:* Do this verbally and in writing especially if the deal is complex or confusing. Encourage the other side to summarize their understanding of the deal. Not only is summarizing appropriate in the closing stage, but when you reach an impasse, it also demonstrates how much progress you have made and may encourage future progress. If nothing else, describe the process, "We certainly have gotten a lot of good ideas on the table today." "I know if we just work at it, we have the right people to get this done!"

Team Seating

- *Description:* Arranging your team to communicate your intended negotiating style: formal, informal, collegial, friendly, adversarial, and so on.
- *Sounds like:* "What's the best way to arrange ourselves around this table?" "Is everyone comfortable?"
- *Advantages:* Fosters the climate you wish to set. Makes it easier to communicate or caucus with your team.
- *Disadvantages:* May be uncomfortable for the other side. Not always within your control.
- *Tips:* The classic pattern is for both lead negotiators to sit across the table from each other, with their respective teams next to them. This makes it easy to confer with your team yet maintain eye contact with the other side. Decide in advance how the room should be set up. If you do plan to alter the seating, make sure you have a reason for doing it; otherwise, it may communicate a different message than you intend.

Testing Questions

- *Description:* Asking a focused question to test the other's position. Also referred to as *arbitrary mirroring*—reflecting back what you have heard in a way that tests the tenacity of the other's position.
- *Sounds like:* "Are you saying there are no other alternatives?" "Do you mean that the entire deal is contingent on this point?" "Is there any information at all that would change your mind?"
- *Advantages:* Checks tenacity without confronting. Buys you time.
- *Disadvantages:* Can backfire if the answer is not what you want. Could sound like a "take-it-or-leave-it" statement.
- *Tips:* Because testing questions encourage the other party to restate their position, they can backfire if the response to your

question is no. However, at least you have tested the firmness of the position. Watch the phrasing of your questions.

Walk-Away

- *Description:* Signaling that no further negotiation is possible unless an immediate concession is made.
- *Sounds like:* "I see that there's no point in continuing." "We're just too far apart at this point. Call me if anything changes."
- *Advantages:* Sends strong signal that deadlock is possible. It is an action step versus doing nothing.
- *Disadvantages:* Could terminate the negotiation. Threatens the relationship.
- *Tips:* Can be used literally or figuratively. You must be prepared to take some action, such as leaving the room or threatening to deadlock, if the other side's offer is worse than your predetermined walk-away point (see *Settlement Range* in Chapter 3). At least, consider calling a caucus. No action on your part signals to the other side that their position is in the acceptable range. Can also be used when the other side engages in personal attacks or emotional outbursts.

Warn—Don't Threaten

- *Description:* Clearly stating the downside of the other side's position or behavior.
- *Sounds like:* "If you keep interrupting, we're never going to get through this." "Here is what we'll have to do if you do X." "I feel I should tell you that if you continue to [behave outrageously, take such a firm position], we'll have to reconsider doing business with you."
- *Advantages:* Alternative to an outright threat. Acknowledges that they are damaging the relationship or impeding the process.
- *Disadvantages:* Can be perceived as a threat.

- *Tips:* Similar to the Walk-Away, you have to determine how far they can push you in their position or behavior. Develop an acceptable BATNA so you can disengage if necessary. There is a subtle distinction between making an outright threat, and telling the other side "what might happen if . . ."

What If? and Would You Consider?

- *Description:* Posing alternatives and options.
- *Sounds like:* "What if we could give you _____ ? Would that help you with _____ ?" "Would you consider alternative financing?"
- *Advantages:* Expands options. Supports brainstorming.
- *Disadvantages:* Takes time. Have to be fast on your feet (or a thorough planner) to come up with alternatives on the spot.
- *Tips:* Serves as a good way to get the other side to reveal more about their limits. "What if we extended the warranty? Would you consider paying the freight yourself?" These are effective ways to expand options. Must be two-way; get the other side to participate.

Zeroing In

- *Description:* Determining what the seller will accept or what the buyer is willing pay. Often involves getting the other party to display their entire rate card and then working toward the lower price.
- *Sounds like:* "You're asking $1.15 per pound for 10,000 pounds, and $1.10 for an order over 20,000 pounds. How about $1.10 for 10,000 pounds?" "Would you consider renting the apartment furnished at that rate?" "I like the terms for the five-year lease, how about if we do that for three years." "Would you give me the 100 GB hard drive for the price of the 75 GB unit?"
- *Advantages:* Allows you to discover more about the other parties pricing, and their settlement range.

- *Disadvantages:* May risk a Walk-Away or a no by the other party. Could be perceived as "dickering" or Nibbling (an adversarial tactic).
- *Tips:* Be sure to compare their offer with your settlement range. Be prepared to make a minor concession on a less important item.

At the beginning of this chapter, we stated that tactics can work to strengthen the relationship or to intimidate, discourage, or even anger and upset the other party. The win-win tactics we just explored provide positive actions you can take to strengthen the relationship and are more likely to ensure a win-win outcome. In Chapter 9, we explore adversarial tactics. Even though we do not encourage you to use these tactics, other negotiators will and you should be prepared with win-win tactics and other actions to counter adversarial measures.

KEY POINTS

☞ Tactics are behaviors—actions used by the negotiator to serve a purpose or to pursue an objective.
☞ Tactics can be skillfully planned or allowed to just happen in the course of a negotiation.
☞ Win-win tactics are more likely to lead to a mutually beneficial agreement.
☞ Adversarial tactics are more likely to put the other party at a disadvantage by intimidating, discouraging, or upsetting them.

Practical Application

Table 8.1 provides a summary list of all the win-win tactics discussed in this chapter. Based on reading this chapter and your negotiation planning, check the win/win tactics you intend to use in your next negotiation.

TABLE 8.1 Win/Win Tactics

Agenda	Mark up the document
Authority limits	Objective criteria
Balancing the scales	Off-the-record discussions
Brainstorming	Patience/persistence
Bundling	Pinch factor
Caucus	Saying no!
Change of pace	Scaling
Change the negotiator	Side memos
Closing the deal	Soak time
Columbo (a.k.a. playing dumb)	Summarizing
Common interests	Team seating
Concessions	Testing questions
Convert the associates	Walk-Away
Create empathy	Warn, don't threaten
Disclosure	"What if . . . would you consider . . ."
Expand the pie	Zeroing in
Face saving techniques	

Adversarial Tactics and Countertactics

*Keeping score of old scores and scars, getting even and one-upping,
always make you less than you are.*

—Malcolm Forbes

Adversarial Tactics

In Chapter 8, we presented win-win tactics that are useful in moving the negotiation to a mutually beneficial agreement and that serve to strengthen the relationship. In this chapter, we describe adversarial tactics, and include countertactics to deal with them.

These are tactics that would most likely cause you some difficulty or damage the relationship. Many of these tactics are also referred to as "dirty tricks,"[1] "hardball tactics,"[2] "gambits,"[3] or "competitive tactics."[4] The reason that I present adversarial tactics in this book so that you can recognize and respond to them. I recommend that you do *not* use these tactics if you are interested in reaching win-win agreements.

Similar to the win-win tactics in Chapter 8, these tactics are organized alphabetically and are laid out in the following format:

- *Description:* What the tactic is about.
- *Sounds like:* The words or phrases negotiators use to execute the tactic.
- *Countermeasures:* Specific actions that you can take to deal with the tactic.
- *Recommended win-win countertactics:* Specific positive tactics you can use to off-set the adversarial tactic being used against you.

Each of the following tactics may damage a relationship or prevent a win-win outcome:

142

Authority Escalation

- *Description:* Introducing a new person or an additional approval step in the negotiation. Escalating authority tactics are designed to wear out the other side—both physically and psychologically.
- *Sounds like:* "This sound fine to me, let me run it by the sales manager." "Now, if I can just get the committee to sign off on this, I think we have a deal."
- *Countermeasures:* Raise the issue early! Toward the end of the negotiation, be prepared for last-minute authority changes. Test it. Ask them to describe their authority as clearly as possible. Know their organization; reporting structure and how they operate.
- *Recommended win-win countertactics:* Authority Limits, Change the Negotiator, Testing Questions, Walk-Away.

Bluffing/Lying

- *Description:* Deliberately lying or misrepresenting a position.
- *Sounds like:* "I can get a much better price from your competitor." "There are plenty of other people just waiting for a deal like this." "There's another offer, if you don't take it."
- *Countermeasures:* Don't attack the person; instead, use Face-Saving Techniques. A good countertactic involves saying: "You know if I had that price and those terms, I would go with Company Y [the competitor] as well. Are you sure we're comparing apples to apples here?"
- *Recommended win-win countertactics:* Columbo, Face-Saving Techniques, Objective Criteria.

Cherry-Picking

- *Description:* Getting multiple bids, and then trying to get the best or lowest offer on each item by playing one supplier against the others. Suppose Supplier A gives the best price; Supplier B gives the best terms; and Supplier C gives the best warranty. The buyer starts the next round of negotiation by asking each supplier to make a proposal at A's price, B's terms, and C's warranty.

- *Sounds like:* "I like your price, but Supplier B will give me better terms. You'll have to match his terms." "If you give me the same warranty as Supplier C, I think we'll have a deal."
- *Countermeasures:* Make a small concession on price only. Know your competition and have the courage to say no.
- *Recommended win-win countertactics:* Balance the Scales, Bundling, Say No, Caucus, Closing the Deal, Zeroing In.

Crunch Time[5]

- *Description:* Insisting that the other side make an immediate concession to stay in the running. People use it because it works.
- *Sounds like:* "You've got to do better than that." "Why don't you sharpen your pencil and come back with a better offer."
- *Countermeasures:* The best initial response is to find out what the problem is. Unfortunately, the most common response is to make an immediate concession of some type. Explore the resistance.
- *Recommended win-win countertactics:* Saying No, Testing Questions, Balancing the Scales, Closing the Deal, What if ?

Deadline Pressure

- *Description:* Setting a deadline or taking advantage of a deadline.
- *Sounds like:* "We have a strike deadline at midnight." "The price goes up at the end of the month." "The money won't be in the budget after next week."
- *Countermeasures:* Realize that time is power. Limit your disclosures about time pressures. When negotiating overseas, beware of telling the other party when your return flight is scheduled. Deadlines force action and you can use this tac-

tic to your advantage. Don't accept it as fact—negotiate it. Labor negotiators have been known to pull the plug on the clock as a strike deadline approaches.

- *Recommended win-win countertactics:* Close the Deal, Common Interests, What If ?

Deadlock

- *Description:* Realizing that the parties cannot reach agreement. Perhaps the most powerful and uncomfortable tactic and situation to face, a deadlock leaves a negotiator with a sense of failure and requires an unpleasant explanation to others inside your organization.
- *Sounds like:* "Looks like we're at an impasse." "I can't see how we're going to close the gap."
- *Countermeasures:* Neither side wants to deadlock if they truly wanted to reach an agreement. Remember: No deal is better than a bad deal! Review Chapter 5 for additional guidance.
- *Recommended win-win countertactics:* Common Interests, Change the Negotiator, Soak Time, Patience/Persistence, What if ?, Zeroing In.

Divide and Conquer

- *Description:* Involving multiple negotiators who make side deals with various parts of the vendor organization. The procurement manager works with the sales rep to get a better deal on price while the systems manager cuts a side deal with the vendor's development engineer to include some special software or services. Each concession looks small but the aggregate contract may be a bad deal for the vendor.
- *Countermeasures:* Plan and coordinate with all members of your team who will have contact with the customer. Refer back to your settlement range.
- *Recommended win-win countertactics:* Balancing the Scales, Summarizing, Caucus, Convert the Associates.

Emotional Outburst (a.k.a. the Artful Freak-Out)

- *Description:* Someone erupting into anger and usually name calling.
- *Sounds like:* "I can't X%$& believe this . . . !" "This whole thing is a sham . . ."
- *Countermeasures:* Most emotional outbursts during the negotiation are staged to gain some advantage. Many people are uncomfortable with emotional displays and move to placate or make concessions to keep the peace. The most effective way to deal with an emotional outburst is to remain calm. When things settle down, ask the specifics of the problem. If the outburst is real, then you can deal with the issue, not the emotion.
- *Recommended win-win countertactics:* Patience/Persistence, Change the Negotiator, Caucus, Change of Pace, Convert the Associates, Face-Saving, Warn—Don't Threaten.

End Run

- *Description:* Going around the other party, escalating to a higher authority, or proposing that other people need to be brought in.
- *Sounds like:* "Since your boss is the one who makes the decision, let's just go directly to her." "This is bigger than both of us." "It sounds like we need the lawyers in here."
- *Countermeasures:* Make sure you have support above you to ensure that they will not acquiesce and engage with the other party.
- *Recommended win-win countertactics:* Authority Limits, Change the Negotiator, Convert the Associates, Common Interests.

Fait Accompli

- *Description:* Taking a surprise action like adding in delivery, service contract, transfer fee, closing costs, repairs to property, and so on. It works if the other side thinks that it is easier to ask for forgiveness than permission. Often this will be

146

described as a minor issue when, in fact, it may make a major difference.

- *Sounds like:* "So here's the final contact. All you have to do is sign."
- *Countermeasures:* This tends to affect the balance of power or could occur after the deal is signed. It is related to Nibbling. Take the time to review every aspect of the deal.
- *Recommended win-win countertactics:* Summarizing, Caucus (even with yourself), Columbo, and Soak Time.

Funny Money

- *Description:* Presenting cost information to achieve an advantage. Related to Simple Solutions.
- *Sounds like:* "You're asking 20 cents a pound. We'll give you 19 cents. What's a lousy penny?"
- *Countermeasures:* Discipline yourself to convert funny money to real money. Aggregate or disaggregate any numbers to yield a total real money figure. Some salespeople break down a $350 difference in position by saying, "That's less than a dollar a day for a year." True, but it's your dollar.
- *Recommended win-win countertactics:* Columbo, Testing Questions.

Good Guy/Bad Guy

- *Description:* Occurs especially in team negotiations when one person acts tough and unreasonable and their partner acts nice and reasonable. Remember that if the other side is using this on you, neither person is really the good guy. Sometimes, the good guy is present while the bad guy is in the shadows.
- *Sounds like:* "I wish I could do this for you, but you know I could never get this past _____ [e.g., my boss, the committee, credit department]."
- *Countermeasures:* You can react by walking out, protesting, ignoring the bad guy, or using your own bad guy. Humor

can sometimes work "Hey, I know what you're doing. . . . I saw it on television."

- *Recommended win-win countertactics:* Change of Pace, Convert the Associates, Change the Negotiator.

Last and Final Offer

- *Description:* Stating that this is the limit. Related to "take it or leave it"
- *Sounds like:* "This is our final offer." "Here's the bottom line." "This is as low (high) as we can go."
- *Countermeasures:* You can respond by introducing new alternatives, explaining the true cost of deadlock to both of you, and getting angry if appropriate.
- *Recommended win-win countertactics:* Authority Limits, Brainstorming, Closing the Deal, Creating Empathy, Summarizing, Balancing the Scales, Zeroing In.

Missing Man Maneuver

- *Description:* The person with final authority disappears near the end of the negotiation session. It could be a delaying tactic, signaling that they are going to the competition.
- *Sounds like:* "I have to deal with another situation right now. I'll be back as soon as I can."
- *Countermeasures:* You can react by walking out, putting a time limit on your offer, or going higher.
- *Recommended win-win countertactics:* Agenda, Authority Limits, Convert the Associate, Patience/Persistence.

Nibbling

- *Description:* When one party asks for a relatively minor concession or throw-in, typically at the conclusion of the big negotiation. It works. For example, asking for slightly extended payment terms, a less-than-usual down payment, or an extended warranty.

- *Sounds like:* "How about if we throw in the snow tires." "Since we're almost there, how about 45 day terms instead of 30? It's only bookkeeping."
- *Countermeasures:* Resist the tendency to give in. With tactful firmness, you can decline the nibble or trade it for a larger concession.
- *Recommended win-win countertactics:* Agenda, Balance the Scales, Closing the Deal, Mark Up the Document, Side Memos, Zeroing In.

Nonnegotiable Demands

- *Description:* Eliminating an issue from discussion. This tactic is especially effective if the nonnegotiable demands are included with some reasonable demands.
- *Sounds like:* "We will not talk about _____ . That's nonnegotiable!"
- *Countermeasures:* Push back using testing questions. Conduct off the record talks; explain why you feel otherwise; treat the demands as negotiable and suggest alternatives; caucus. Separate nonnegotiable from reasonable demands.
- *Recommended win-win countertactics:* Off-The-Record Discussions, Side Memos, Testing Questions, Walk-Away, What if?.

Personal Attacks

- *Description:* Referring to negative attacks by the other person on you, often at a personal level. Similar to Emotional Outburst.
- *Sounds like:* "You know, if you really knew this business, you'd see that this is a good deal." "Do I need to explain this to you *again?*" "Your deliveries are always late." "Your competitors are doing well in this market. I wonder why?"
- *Countermeasures:* Be calm; try to ignore it. Use humor. Negotiate to end it. If it persists, walk out and protest as loudly and as high up as you can. You *do not* have to take abuse.

- *Recommended win-win countertactics:* Columbo, Disclosure, Create Empathy, Testing Questions, Warn—Don't Threaten, Walk-Away.

Poor Mouthing

- *Description:* Convincing the other side that there is a dollar limit or some other restriction from the organization.
- *Sounds like:* "This is all I've got!" "My budget just won't allow me to do that." "This is the limit I have approval for."
- *Countermeasures:* Test it since budgets are generally flexible. If it is a real constraint, brainstorm and troubleshoot the issue. Disengage and study the problem; change the payment terms; find out who the decision-maker is (who controls the budget), and enlist their support: "What would we have to do to convince your upper management to expand the budget?"
- *Recommended win-win countertactics:* Authority Limits, Brainstorm, Testing Questions, Expand the Pie.

Red Herring

- *Description:* Creating real and imaginary issues. It is intended to dampen your aspiration level by having you deal with a side issue up front. Once the issue is raised and you begin discussing it, the other side retracts the imaginary issues, hoping to set up the feeling that you now owe them a concession.
- *Sounds like:* "Before we get started, we have to determine team composition and adding members to the team." "What about publicity afterwards?"
- *Countermeasures:* Ignore the issue or table it until later. Concentrate on what issues are most important to you. When the other side raises an issue, be prepared to raise one yourself.
- *Recommended win-win countertactics:* Agenda, Caucus, Scaling.

Rules

- *Description:* Establishing up front ground rules or procedures (e.g., tape recording, seating arrangements, when questions may be asked, order of speaking, caucus periods, team changes, press contact).
- *Sounds like:* "I propose that we limit each session to two hours." "Once the teams are in place, there are no substitutions."
- *Countermeasures:* Some rules can create an advantage for the other side. Like anything else, rules are negotiable. Be alert if the other side proposes or suggests a rule.
- *Recommended win-win countertactics:* Agenda, Brainstorming, Concessions, Off-the-Record discussions.

Simple Solutions

- *Description:* Rounding a number up or down, usually to the proposing side's advantage. People like simplicity, and when you are close to an agreement, it is easy to fall into this trap.
- *Sounds like:* After accepting an offer of $101,500, the buyer says, "I can't remember complicated numbers; how about we round it down to $100,000."
- *Countermeasures:* Stop! Realize the extent of the concession they are asking you to make. Reopen the other currencies included in the deal.
- *Recommended win-win countertactics:* Patience/Persistence, Saying No, Columbo, Closing the Deal.

Split the Difference

- *Description:* When the parties are close to agreement, one side offers to meet you halfway.
- *Sounds like:* "Your offer is X; mine is X + 4; let's split the difference at X + 2? What do you say? That's fair!"
- *Countermeasures:* It is hard to say no because this appears to be so reasonable. After all, it is simple and both sides appear

to be making the same concession. If splitting the difference makes the agreement unacceptable, simply say no.

- *Recommended win-win countertactics:* Saying No, Walk-Away, Objective Criteria, Pinch Factor, Zeroing In.

Surprises

- *Description:* Presenting an issue or using a tactic (e.g., delaying or changing team members) that seems to come out of left field. It is intended to put pressure on you.
- *Sounds like:* "Let's get our Toledo office to review this." "I should probably mention . . ."
- *Countermeasures:* Stop! Think! Listen! Caucus until you can prepare.
- *Recommended win-win countertactics:* Agenda, Caucus, Columbo, Disclosure, Off-The-Record Discussions, Saying No.

Take It or Leave It

- *Description:* Signaling that the other side has reached their limit and doesn't want to haggle any more. At the end of a negotiation, this is a Last and Final Offer approach. The phrase itself is inflammatory.
- *Sounds like:* "That's as far as we go, take it or leave it!"
- *Countermeasures:* Develop a BATNA in advance. Know your power and alternatives.
- *Recommended win-win countertactics:* Caucus, Balancing the Scales, Expand the Pie, Common Interests, Walk-Away.

Threats

- *Description:* Promising to take some punitive action if the other person does not concede. Every negotiation involves a degree of threat.
- *Sounds like:* "If you don't meet my price, I'll give 100 percent of my business to your competitor."

- *Countermeasures:* Threats usually lead to counterthreats. Threats can be real or imaginary. Treat them as real if the other side has other alternatives and can live without you. They may be bluffing. Consider protesting to higher management. Prove that the threat can't hurt you; be irrational; show the person threatening that they have more to lose.
- *Recommended win-win countertactics:* Walk-Away, Warn—Don't Threaten, Caucus.

Without a doubt, if you believe in striving for a win-win outcome, you will stay with win-win tactics. However, you need to be prepared with countermeasures in the event the other side employs adversarial tactics.

KEY POINTS

☞ Adversarial tactics create a climate that tends to damage relationships and to impede a mutually beneficial agreement.

☞ These tactics are often used to intimidate, discourage, or anger the other party.

☞ Adversarial tactics are not recommended, but you should know how to use win-win tactics and other countermeasures to deal with them.

Practical Application

Table 9.1 provides a summary list of all the adversarial tactics discussed in this chapter. Based on reading this chapter and your experience, check the adversarial tactics that have been used on you, or are likely to cause trouble for you.

TABLE 9.1   Adversarial Tactics

Authority escalation	Last and final offer
Bluffing/lying	Missing man maneuver
Cherry picking	Nibbling
Crunch time	Nonnegotiable demands
Deadline pressure	Personal attack
Deadlock	Poor mouthing
Divide and conquer	Red herring
Emotional outburst (a.k.a.	Rules
the artful freak-out)	Simple solutions
End run	Split the difference
Fait accompli	Surprises
Funny money	Take it or leave it
Good guy/bad guy	Threats

10

Tactical Orientation

To be trusted is a greater compliment than to be loved.

—George MacDonald

How to Determine
Your Tactical Orientation

Now that we have a handle on negotiation tactics and countertactics, the next set of questions emerge:

- How will I approach this negotiation?
- Will my behavior (tactics) involve win-win, adversarial, or some combination?
- What behavior (tactics) can I expect from the other side?
- How should I behave and respond?

Every negotiation is different, and the tactics used in one negotiation may not be appropriate for another. When both the issues and the relationship are important, we tend to use win-win tactics. When the relationship is less important, we have a greater range of tactics to choose from. Compare a used car negotiation to one with a colleague at work. With so many negotiating tactics to choose from, how do you know which ones to use *in each negotiation?* Determining your tactical orientation will provide you with general guidance in selecting the tactics consistent with your objectives and your intent. To assess your tactical orientation, ask yourself the following key questions:

- Do I trust them? Do they trust me?
- Am I under time pressure? Are they?
- Is reaching a win/win agreement desirable?

- Am I open to alternative outcomes? Are they?
- Do I want a long-term relationship? Do they?

Key Questions Expanded

- *Do I trust them? Do they trust me?* Think about the people you negotiate with on a regular basis, including coworkers, key clients, vendors, spouse, and family members. Because of your history with these people, you should have a good grasp of how much you trust each other. However, trust is very difficult to assess when you are dealing with a person for the first time. Consider information as a currency—one that is valuable to both sides. Ask yourself, "Is this person forthcoming with information? Do they play it close to the vest? Can I trust the information they give me, or do I need to verify it? How do they treat the information I provide to them? Do they use it to threaten or pressure?" If I disclose to the other party that I am facing a certain deadline, do they use that information to pressure me into a quick decision?

- *Am I under time pressure? Are they?* Time pressure or lack of it can affect the tactics you use. If I have little time, I am more likely to consider a take-it-or-leave-it approach. If the person is not willing to engage or takes a hard line, I need to know that so I can move on to another source to get my needs met. When time is short, I may present an opening position closer to my settlement expectation. However, if I have more time, I may be more patient in waiting out the other party. Ask yourself, "Who is putting time pressure on me? The other side? My management? Someone on my side? How can I reduce this pressure? Can I negotiate the deadline?"

- *Is reaching a win-win agreement desirable?* If I believe in working toward a mutually beneficial agreement for both sides, I am more likely to choose only win-win tactics. Similarly, the other side will respond in kind, if they share the same objective. As the level of complexity in the negotiation increases, it may

157

require extensive implementation. In a divorce, there may be issues of child rearing, property settlements, custody, education, and other long-term issues. With a customer, a complex application may require a more collaborative negotiation to handle implementation pitfalls. To fully implement such agreements, it may be necessary to seek a win-win outcome rather than vanquishing the other party. Conversely, there are numerous stories in construction about low-bid contractors who then make substantial profits through change orders. Trust may be an issue and the contract administrator has to stay vigilant to the legitimacy of such changes.

- *Am I open to alternative outcomes? Are they?* Can I be flexible in accepting alternatives other than the position that I stated initially? As a department manager who wants an additional employee, am I open to a temporary employee or consultant? Would a loan from another department or outsourcing the work meet my needs? In sales or purchasing, can I accept an alternative product or some other method of solving the problem? Am I open to leasing as well as purchasing outright?

- *Do I want a long-term relationship? Do they?* Is it in my best interest to maintain a long-term relationship with the other party? If so, I may decide to make some concessions in this negotiation for the sake of goodwill. Are they interested in a long-term relationship? Ask yourself, "What value would the other party see in a long-term relationship with me? What could I do for them?" Increasingly, companies are entering into partnering relationships with suppliers because of the mutual benefit of steady supply and demand. A long-term relationship also enhances trust and ensures a more collaborative negotiation.

Tactical Orientation Continuum

How can we put the previous questions to work? Think of a continuum with one end representing the win-win zone and the other end the adversarial tactics zone. The middle is the neutral zone (see Figure 10.1).

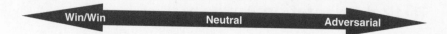

FIGURE 10.1 Tactical Orientation Continuum

Next, answer each of the questions in Figure 10.2 using the following scale:

+2 Definitely yes

+1 Possible yes

 0 Unsure

−1 Possible no

−2 Definitely no

- Do I trust them? _____   Do they trust me? _____

- Am I under time pressure? _____   Are they? _____

- Is reaching a win/win agreement desirable? _____   To them? _____

- Am I open to alternative outcomes? _____   Are they? _____

- Do I want a long-term relationship? _____   Do they? _____

My Score: _____   Their Score: _____

Win/Win					Neutral				Adversarial	
+10	+8	+6	+4	+2	0	−2	−4	−6	−8	−10

- In which "Zone" am I? _____

- In which "Zone" are they? _____

FIGURE 10.2 Tactical Orientation Questions and Continuum

159

Tactical Orientation Analysis

Are you surprised at where you ended up on the continuum? How about the other side? If so, look back at the questions to see which items you assigned a 0 or a minus number. Ask yourself:

In which zone (i.e., win-win, adversarial, or neutral) am I?

In which zone (i.e., win-win, adversarial, or neutral) are they?

Determine if changing any of these items would enhance the negotiation. If you discovered that the other party did not trust you, what are some gestures or behaviors that you could exhibit to prove trustworthy to the other side? Perhaps, disclosing some in-depth information about your needs could work to build trust.

If you are under time pressure, what can you do to relieve it? Many union negotiations have a midnight strike deadline to put pressure on both sides to reach an agreement. Sometimes, negotiators will literally stop the clock; in one instance, by pulling the plug from the wall. In terms of a win-win outcome, how could you go beyond just the issues on the table to expand the pie so that a win is possible for both sides? Consider the loan processing case from Chapter 2 where the director of loan processing agreed to serve as an advocate for the IT department in the next budget round.

Finally, if a long-term relationship is important to you but not necessarily important to the other side, what can you do to enhance the importance of the relationship to them? Think about it from their perspective. What could you do so that *they need you as much as you need them*? How about serving as a reference for them to other customers? Or providing them with referrals? When dealing with a car dealership, offer to return to them each time you need to buy a new car. This works as a win-win since you get a better buying experience and perhaps a better price, and they get a quality used car as your trade-in and another sale. Offer to bring your friends and family. Ask for a specific salesperson. As one car salesman, put it "Make a friend and sell a car."

How does placing yourself and the other side on the tactical orientation continuum help determine how you and they will act in the negotiation? Below are some suggested actions for each zone:

Win-Win Zone Actions

- Use win-win or cooperative tactics exclusively.
- Work hard to identify and satisfy *their needs* as well as my own.
- Disclose information in an open manner.
- Trust the information they share with me.

Adversarial Zone Actions

- Watch for adversarial tactics by the other side.
- Use win-win tactics to counter.
- Be careful to ensure that any concessions do not undermine my needs.
- Disclose little information unless reciprocated.
- Verify the information they share with me.

Neutral Zone Actions

- Use win-win or cooperative tactics to set the tone.
- Watch for signs of adversarial tactics.
- Disclose information in a limited manner; ask for reciprocity.
- Trust the information they share with me to some extent.

Tactical Selection

After determining the zone that you and the other side are likely to occupy, what specific tactics should you select? What can you anticipate from the other side? Ask yourself:

- Based on my tactical orientation, what tactics will I use?
- What zone do I assume the other side is in?
- If adversarial, what can I do to convert the situation toward the neutral or win-win zone?
- What tactics do I think the other side will use? How will I respond?

Table 10.1 shows the stage in which tactics are most likely to be used. Consider this table as a guide. The use of various tactics may occur at any of the stages. Even though the win-win and adversarial tactics are lined up next to each other, the best countermeasure for each adversarial tactic is found in Chapter 9.

KEY POINTS

☞ *Tactical orientation* refers to a process that will provide you with general guidance in selecting tactics consistent with your objectives and intent.

☞ Key questions to determine your tactical orientation:
—Do I trust them? Do they trust me?
—Am I under time pressure? Are they?
—Is reaching a win-win agreement desirable?
—Am I open to alternative outcomes? Are they?
—Do I want a long-term relationship? Do they?

☞ By assigning values to this series of questions, you can determine your tactical orientation.

☞ The tactical orientation continuum contains three zones:
—*Win-win zone:* Where win-win tactics are likely to be used.
—*Neutral zone:* Where a mixture of win-win and adversarial tactics are likely to be used.
—*Adversarial zone:* Where adversarial tactics are likely to be used.

☞ *Tactical selection* involves selecting the specific tactics you plan to use and to anticipate what tactics the other side may use, based on tactical orientation.

TABLE 10.1 Tactics by Stage

Stage	Win-Win Zone Tactics	Adversarial Zone Tactics
Opening		
Set the climate and agenda	Agenda	Missing man maneuver
	Common interests	Deadline pressure
Establish the process	Disclosure	Personal attacks
State and respond to opening positions	Authority limits	Rules
	Team seating	Good guy/Bad guy
	Columbo	Red herring
	Objective criteria	Poor mouthing
	Saying no	Crunch time
	Walk-Away	Nonnegotiable demands
Exploring		
Distinguish between wants and needs	Create empathy	Bluffing/Lying
	Expand the pie	Cherry-picking
Identify alternative currencies/options	Scaling	Divide and conquer
	Testing questions	End run
Match currencies to needs	Brainstorming	Funny money
	Bundling	Split the difference
	What if . . .?	Surprises
	Balancing the scales	Take it or leave it
	Concessions	Threats
	Patience/Persistence	
	Soak time	
	Warn, don't threaten	
	Zeroing in	
Closing		
Summarize the agreement and contract	Caucus	Authority escalation
	Change of pace	Deadlock
Communicate and implement	Closing the deal	Fait accompli
	Mark up the document	Last and final offer
	Pinch factor	Nibbling
	Side memos	Simple solutions
	Summarizing	Split the difference

Practical Application

+2	Definitely yes
+1	Possible yes
0	Unsure
−1	Possible no
−2	Definitely no

- Do I trust them? _____   Do they trust me? _____
- Am I under time pressure? _____   Are they? _____
- Is reaching a win/win agreement desirable? _____   To them? _____
- Am I open to alternative outcomes? _____   Are they? _____
- Do I want a long-term relationship? _____   Do they? _____

My Score: _____   Their Score: _____

Win/Win					Neutral				Adversarial	
+10	+8	+6	+4	+2	0	−2	−4	−6	−8	−10

- In which "Zone" am I? _____
- In which "Zone" are they? _____

FIGURE 10.3 **Tactical Orientation Questions and Scale**

TABLE 10.2 Tactics by Stage

Stage	Win-Win Zone Tactics	Adversarial Zone Tactics
Opening		
Set the climate and agenda	Agenda	Missing man maneuver
	Common interests	Deadline pressure
Establish the process	Disclosure	Personal attacks
State and respond to opening positions	Authority limits	Rules
	Team seating	Good guy/Bad guy
	Columbo	Red herring
	Objective criteria	Poor mouthing
	Saying no	Crunch time
	Walk-Away	Nonnegotiable demands
Exploring		
Distinguish between wants and needs	Create empathy	Bluffing/Lying
	Expand the pie	Cherry-picking
Identify alternative currencies/options	Scaling	Divide and conquer
	Testing questions	End run
Match currencies to needs	Brainstorming	Funny money
	Bundling	Split the difference
	What if . . .?	Surprises
	Balancing the scales	Take it or leave it
	Concessions	Threats
	Patience/Persistence	
	Soak time	
	Warn, don't threaten	
	Zeroing in	
Closing		
Summarize the agreement and contract	Caucus	Authority escalation
	Change of pace	Deadlock
Communicate and implement	Closing the deal	Fait accompli
	Mark up the document	Last and final offer
	Pinch factor	Nibbling
	Side memos	Simple solutions
	Summarizing	Split the difference

Special Negotiation Situations

Most people in the U.S. think goods have a fixed price and that it would be inappropriate to suggest bargaining for one which is lower. Yet three-quarters of the world population buy and sell merchandize without a fixed price. The value of goods is determined through negotiation between buyer and seller.

—Robert A. Maddux

Negotiating in Buy and Sell Situations

Earlier in the book, we focused on the multiple currencies that salespeople can use in negotiating with customers. In addition, we acknowledged that many people in customer-facing situations underestimate their power. In buy and sell situations, there are increasing pressures from buyers such as commoditizing your products or services, reverse auctions, gray markets, and increasing competitive leverage. In this chapter, we explore some specific techniques that people in selling situations can use to help make the deal and sustain the relationship:

- *Focus on value not on price.* Consider the old story about the alligator and the bear. In a fight between a grizzly bear and an alligator, the terrain determines the victor. The grizzly bear would win a fight on land, but the alligator would win if the fight moved to the water. The lesson for business is to keep the fight on your own turf. Negotiating on price places the fight in the customer's win zone. Value, however, favors the supplier. Purchasing agents are famous for squeezing suppliers on price. Look at the tactics of the big-box stores in gaining price concessions based on volume. In interview-

168

ing numerous salespeople, they all attest to the fact that value can only be perceived at a level high enough in the organization to appreciate the value proposition.

- *Develop the full value proposition.* Consider all of the currencies we reviewed in Chapter 4, especially those in complex sales. Successful value propositions include extensive currencies and use the value proposition pyramid (Figure 11.1).

  Most salespeople are aware of initial cost (IC) and total cost of ownership (TCOO), but human and business impacts (HABI) may represent a new thought. I first learned about HABI in a seminar on how to sell lighting products.[1] The instructor asked us to look beyond IC and TCOO to consider the HABI of lighting. As a class, we analyzed HABI and discovered that lighting has a discernable impact on employee productivity, safety, morale, and work space aesthetics. Consider the cost of a law suit based on a slip and fall

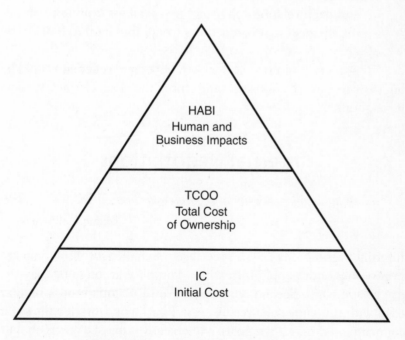

FIGURE 11.1 Value Proposition Pyramid

accident. When we actually put dollar amounts to HABI, the impact of the value proposition increased remarkably. To enhance your value proposition, think about how you could position your products and services based on HABI.

- *Continue to develop a broad-based customer relationship.* In managing major accounts, focusing on the development of broad relationships in the customer space is essential. A single point of contact, such as a purchasing manager, leaves the salesperson vulnerable to price-focused negotiating. Worse yet, what happens if that person leaves? You may be stuck negotiating with someone who has a favored vendor, but it's not you. In similar fashion, invite and encourage others in your organization to get involved in the buyer-seller interface to ensure that a tighter relationship between the *companies* is established. Terry Bacon in *Selling to Major Accounts* refers to this as "building a zippered net . . . with important connections occurring up and down the line."[2] Such broad and deep relationships build partnerships leading to strategic alliances that competitors would find hard to break.

These suggestions work for both buyer and seller and could be built into the relationship and into the negotiating process throughout.

Internal Negotiations

Nothing, of course, begins at the time you think it did.
—Lillian Hellman

Internal negotiations pose a special set of challenges. First, you are negotiating with people with whom you have an ongoing, day-to-day relationship. Second, you may have to negotiate on a regular basis with the same resource owners. Third, you work for the same company, so the strategy, goals, and objectives may be common, but the resources allocated to achieve these are not.

170

The concept of internal negotiation also applies to sales or customer-facing individuals. Remember the equation 1E = 3I? For each external deal with a customer, there are usually three internal negotiations with resource owners.

All of the models, techniques, and tactics that we have presented thus far can be applied to both internal and external negotiations. However, in internal negotiations, developing your influence skills can help immensely. A complete treatment of influence skills that are useful in internal negotiations is found in *Influence without Authority* by Bradford and Cohen.[3] In this book, the authors list numerous currencies and skills useful to internal negotiators.

The challenges described earlier can foster organizational gridlock or lead to higher quality win-win outcomes if the following general guidelines are used:

- *Highlight areas of agreement at the beginning and throughout the negotiation.* Consider how much common ground the parties share and acknowledge it. Underscore previous agreements that have led to success in meeting departmental and organizational objectives. I recall two telecommunications field technicians negotiating (more like arguing) about who was going to go out in a snowstorm to adjust an antenna. After 10 minutes of back and forth exchange, one technician grabbed the other's ID badge, then his own and said: "You've got one of these. I've got one of these. Let's just stop this and get out there and fix that antenna."

- *Convert the situation from a "me versus you" to an "us against the problem" approach.* In Chapter 2, we introduced the loan processing case where the loan processing manager requested a programming change from the IT manager. By successfully focusing on the problem, they came to a solution that not only satisfied the immediate needs (i.e., the reprogramming was done by college interns, and the IT manager kept the integrity of the project management queue), but also solved longer term issues such as IT's resource constraints due to budget cuts and the long queue

171

for users. By focusing on the problem, a true win-win resulted.

- *Use facts and logic sparingly.* If resistance occurs, use questioning and listening to understand the other party's point of view. Facts and logic will only take you so far in a discussion where there is conflict. If a dispute can be resolved through logical argument, it is more likely that you are problem solving than negotiating. Draw the other person out by asking questions that focus on *their* needs, such as: "What impact would this have on your schedule? Tell me more about your budget constraints?"

- *Offer currencies beyond the issue being negotiated.* As we saw in many of the internal cases in previous chapters, resistance is often a function of resource constraints. No one comes to work wanting to disappoint their colleagues or internal customers. When you discover the source of the resistance, explore beyond the initial push-back to expose the underlying problem. The resistance is usually people, time, or money. Find a way to offer future support to enhance their position in obtaining the resources needed to serve their internal customers. As a customer, you have more leverage than you think. In terms of elegant currencies, your offer may be as simple as helping them create a business case for more resources, or attending a meeting to support an increase in their budget.

- *Avoid inflating your wants and needs.* Anyone who has been through a budget cycle in an organization knows that there is a certain amount of inflation that occurs in presenting a position. However, if your organization is like most, those around the table know if your demands are out of line. In similar fashion, when negotiating internally, trust is a significant issue. If you play the sky-is-falling card too often, especially if you cite customer crises, your credibility might be shot. Remember the rule of an opening position—make it high, but defensible.

- *Resist escalation.* In most organizations today, decision making is being driven down to the lowest level. Consider higher authority as your last resort. Try to resolve the dispute at your level. Involve peers if you think they can help you gain perspective. Escalation not only reduces your power, but also damages relationships all around you, especially with your boss.

Hallway Negotiations

Internal negotiations involve some special characteristics, and we are often unaware that we're involved in a negotiation. In hallway negotiations,[4] two conditions must be met: (1) The request by one party creates a conflict for the other (e.g., schedule, staffing, priorities), and (2) neither of the parties has authority over the other—or chooses not to use it. Consider the following common situations:

- A colleague wants to exchange a vacation week with you.
- You ask a fellow manager for the loan of a staff person for a few hours or a few days.
- Your boss wants you to take her place at a steering committee meeting.

Any one of these situations could create a conflict if you have a full schedule, deadlines, and demands. So, how do you operate in this environment? Persuading with facts and logic doesn't seem to work. The other side has just as many reasons not to do it. Consider what the other person is asking for. What's the underlying need? Can you provide it in some other way? With some other resource? At some other time? If you are not sure of what to say, disengage until you can assess the impact on your workload and priorities. Think about what your needs are and see if the other party can provide you a currency to meet your needs. Here's an example:

JOHN: Mary, I need a favor.
MARY: What's that?
JOHN: Could you cover for me at the executive committee next week? It will take most of the morning on Thursday.

MARY: Next week! That's when my team is putting together the proposal for the Giant Company project. It's also due at the end of next week.

JOHN: It sounds like we're both in a time bind.

MARY: Yeah, that's true. I'm sorry but there's no way I can do it.

JOHN: You mentioned that you're working on Giant Company. Jorge in my department has lots of really good information on that company and could help your people in shaping the proposal. Would that help?

MARY: Yes. That would be great. Can he meet with us today?

JOHN: How about tomorrow first thing? I'll have him pull together some information and be ready by then.

MARY: Great! And I'll cover the executive committee for you next Thursday.

None of us likes to turn down a colleague, but we have our own workload, priorities, and other needs as well. Sharing information and resources helps us discover ways to meet each others needs.

Negotiating with Your Boss

One of the most common internal negotiation situations involves your boss. Picture yourself sitting in your office Friday afternoon with a full plate. The company's downsizing has left you with fewer resources to get it all done; budget constraints and a headcount freeze do nothing to help.

Now your boss comes to you and says, "I know you're loaded down right now, but I need this project done by Monday. I wish I could give you more time, but Pat is really hot on this. You've always come through for me before, and I know I can depend on you."

You feel frustrated. These new demands mean that you'll be unable to do your best. You won't be able to finish other projects in time, which means not only disappointing clients, but also putting yourself at risk with the boss for failure to deliver.

What do you do? You know you're overloaded. You may feel anger or frustration, but what good does that do? So you work eight hours over the weekend, missing time with your family and an event you'd planned to attend. On Monday, you submit a really good draft, which then sits on your boss' desk until Friday, when the boss finally reviews it, and then wants all the changes made by the following Monday.

What will you say this time? You know what you'd like to say! But that might cost you the job you otherwise enjoy. What did you say? Was it, "Well, I'll fit it in somehow"? Did you feel that you couldn't say no because you wanted to look good? Did you think caving in was the only option? Or was it fear of losing your job? Did you end up accepting an additional project knowing that everything else, including your personal life, would suffer?

If the answer to any of these questions is yes, some helpful suggestions follow. These tips may help you manage tasks and projects, do a good job, and not feel constantly behind schedule. We begin by breaking the problem into its components, and then give you six practical tips you can use when negotiating with your boss.[5]

Looking at Tasks

Every task can be broken down into three factors:

1. *Specification:* What someone wants done.
2. *Time:* How long it takes to do it.
3. *Resources:* What is needed to get it done.

Specification can be verbal or written, a casual request or a detailed description complete with deliverables and quality standards. *Time* may first involve a rough mental estimate or a detailed step-by-step flow chart or schedule. *Resources* include items like budget, staff, computer or equipment access, raw materials, or information.

If you're like most people, when a task is specified, you make mental and sometimes written estimates of the time it will take you to do it, and the equipment, money, people, and information you'll need to get it done. A task doesn't exist in a vacuum. You have other tasks ongoing (some urgent), and you'll have to adjust the time and resources you've allocated to those tasks and somehow fit in this one.

The Triangle

Perhaps the best way of visualizing the situation is with a triangle, as shown in Figure 11.2.

It is up to you, as the person taking on the task or project, to determine the length of the sides of this triangle. Once you've estimated the task, you can apply the *Rule of the Triangle*, which states that the *area must remain proportional*. This means that any *change* to one side means an *adjustment* to one or both of the other sides.

Let's assume that your boss assigns you a new project. You estimate it will take you 10 days to complete with two assistants. But your boss insists that it be done in five days. Your boss is cutting the *time* leg of the triangle in half.

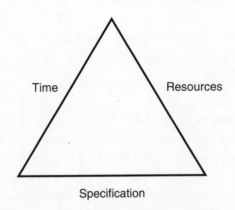

FIGURE 11.2   Specification-Time-Resources Triangle

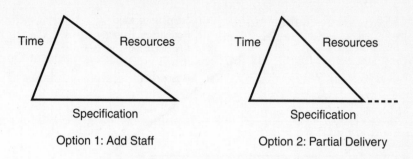

FIGURE 11.3 **Adjusting the Triangle**

The only way you can meet this deadline and retain the area of the triangle is to adjust one or both of the other legs—*resources* or *specification* (see Figure 11.3).

You have two options: (1) you can add staff, or (2) you can offer partial delivery. You must get your boss to change the specifications. You can learn more by playing with the diagram, remembering that an adjustment to *one* side requires additional adjustments (see Figures 11.4 through 11.7).

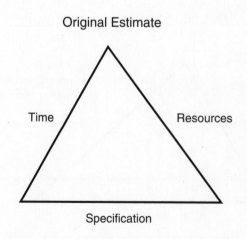

FIGURE 11.4 **Triangle: Original Estimate**

177

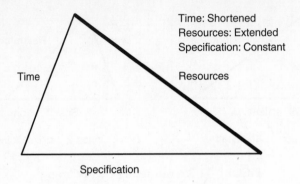

FIGURE 11.5   Triangle: (Adjusted)

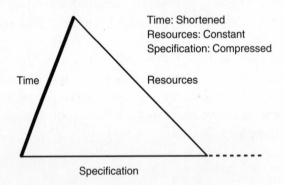

FIGURE 11.6   Triangle: (Adjusted)

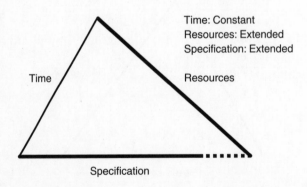

FIGURE 11.7   Triangle: (Adjusted)

Handling the Situation

To build your capability to function effectively under such pressures, you have to learn to negotiate with your boss, clients, or anyone who needs your time and expertise. These six practical steps can help you negotiate project assignments without feeling that you are constantly overloaded and behind schedule:

1. *Allow a reasonable time for a quality job.* Tim is a brilliant design engineer working in a medium-sized firm. Tim often promises designs in an attempt to please his company's clients and frustrates himself by not leaving enough time to meet his own standards. Lately, many of Tim's designs required redrafting because of sloppy work. When he does get it right, he is often late in delivery. He sets the deadlines! What's the problem?

   Tim is inclined to overestimate his ability to deliver. Become a tough and realistic estimator. Restrain your optimism. Make accurate estimates of what it takes to do a job, and then don't commit yourself beyond your capabilities.

2. *Determine the specifications.* With either boss or client, take the time to determine what it is they want. It may not be immediately obvious. You may have to ask questions to get to the heart of the matter. Don't let diffidence or shyness get in the way.

   Take Jane's case. Jane generates several key management reports each month. Her boss recently requested an additional summary report. Reluctant to appear ignorant, or to press her boss too closely, Jane gleaned a superficial understanding of what the boss wanted and then worked for a month to reprogram the system. When she presented the new report format, the boss replied, "This is interesting, but not at all what I expected!" It took Jane several iterations to get it right.

   Jane could have saved herself all of this wasted work by asking the boss to specify clearly what the new report format should look like. She also would have made a better impression by getting it right the first time.

179

3. *Build in a contingency reserve.* Give yourself room to adapt to changing conditions. For instance, a person you thought could work with you may have been pulled off the project suddenly, or the task may have taken longer than you expected. Most people fail to build in any slack and therefore are forced to renegotiate. If you include a contingency in your plan, you will save a great deal of frustration, and you may even be able to deliver early or under budget.

4. *Use resources creatively.* Your company's priorities change daily. Projects get dropped, added, reprioritized, or accelerated. If change occurs, you have the right to revise the estimate and ask for more time or resources. Provide options to your boss or internal clients, such as changing the schedule or getting some outside temporary help for the short-term overload. Use the triangle to think it through or to explain it to your boss.

5. *Know which factor drives the project.* Often, one or more of a project's components is fixed and cannot be changed. We can speak of these as fixed factor projects. Some examples include:

   • Specification-fixed tasks cannot be changed, but time and resources can be adjusted. Fran is a quality controller at a large pharmaceutical laboratory. Because her vaccines must meet the highest standards of purity and quality, specification is the unbending factor.

   • Time-fixed tasks are deadline driven. Fred, a manufacturing manager at a major brewery, agreed to do a special run for a sales promotion on Super Bowl weekend. With a fixed deadline, he estimated the machine time too tightly. One of the four production lines went down and several key markets did not receive the product to coincide with the company's advertising campaign. As a consequence, Fred lost his job.

   • Resource-fixed tasks are keyed to the availability of money, staff, or other resources. Miguel works in human resources for a manufacturing company. He can take as long as he likes with some projects, provided he stays within budget and does not use outside consultants.

Once you know which factor is fixed, you can adjust the others. If the task is specification-fixed, you can ask for more time, more resources, or both. If it is time-fixed, you can either offer partial fulfillment, thus changing the specification, or you can ask for more resources. If the task is resource-fixed, you again can seek to change the specification or you can extend the time.

6. *Learn to say "Yes, and . . ." rather than "No."* Instead of saying "No," say "Yes, and here's what the cost or impact will be . . ." In other words, test the deadline or budget constraints. How strong are they? How much give is there? You may be surprised.

- *Test specification:* "If we can't give you a final draft with firm figures, can we deliver a preliminary draft with estimated numbers?"

- *Test time:* "Are you saying there is no way we can extend this deadline?"

- *Test resources:* "Are there any conditions under which you would agree to pay for outside help on this?"
  Use "if-then" trade-offs. Offer something else in return for what you ask. Here are a few examples:
  — Specification-fixed tasks: "If you go from three to four colors on the layout, the quality will improve dramatically. However, it will cost you an additional $300 in printing and two hours of set up time."
  — Time-fixed tasks: "If you can extend the schedule one more day, then we can deliver the extra 3,000 units."
  — Resource-fixed tasks: "If I can subcontract the magazine assembly, then I can guarantee high-quality results— on time."

Example: Before and After

The following is an example of an employee negotiating with her boss, before and after learning negotiating skills:

Before

BOSS: Sharon, I need you in Pittsburgh tomorrow to investigate the Apco claim.

EMPLOYEE: But, Frank, I'm already working on several claims in Florida right now. You remember, that was last week's fire!

BOSS: I wish it could be different; you'll just have to squeeze it in somehow! Let me know how it goes.

EMPLOYEE: [Frustrated] Why is it always like this, Frank? I guess I have no choice, but this is really going to be a stretch.

BOSS: I promise I'll never do it to you again, Promise!

EMPLOYEE: Yeah!

After

BOSS: Sharon, I need you in Pittsburgh tomorrow to investigate the Apco claim.

EMPLOYEE: It sounds like that's top priority. As you know, I'm working on several Florida claims right now. But, if you really need me in Pittsburgh, I have several suggestions: Assign an extra person to Florida, and alert the Pittsburgh office that I'll need a local person to work with me tomorrow. (Expand resources.)

BOSS: That might work, but you said you had several ideas.

EMPLOYEE: If the extra resources aren't available, then slip the schedule on the Florida tasks for another week. (Extend the schedule.)

BOSS: We could, but all these jobs are critical.

EMPLOYEE: Okay, Frank, the only other time I have is serving on the Standardization Task Force. You could assign that to someone else. (Change specification or task.)

BOSS: Okay, let me check out these options. I'll call you in half an hour.

[half an hour later]

BOSS: I put John on the Task Force; let me know how it goes in Pittsburgh. Deal?

EMPLOYEE: Deal! I'll keep you posted.

Notice what this employee did. She had a problem. She discovered that her boss wanted her to do something that exceeded her available time and resources. Sharon offered her boss several options to get the task done.

You can adapt this to your situation. Ask if you can reschedule the projects that you're now working on. Is that acceptable? If it is, you have extended your time line so that you don't get caught short with the limited resources you now have. If your boss insists that all projects be done on time, ask for more resources to cover the additional drain the new project puts on your present resource pool. If neither time nor resources can be adjusted, then you must ask the boss to take back one or more of the projects that you've already been given and reassign them to someone else.

What you're actually saying to your boss is "Yes, I can do it and here's what it will cost. Either we must slip the schedule, or it will cost you additional resources, or it will cost you on the specification side by shifting the other projects I'm working on."

To negotiate properly, you need information. First, determine what the boss or client wants (specification). Break the project down according to its fixed and flexible components. Use the concept of the triangle diagram to think it through. Then, make realistic estimates of how long the task would take (time) if nothing changed and how changing any of the factors would affect the outcome.

State a clear time frame to the boss. You should be able to say, "I've estimated that the project will take me three weeks with the resources I now have." State a definite period and remind the boss of the other project commitments you have. Review the necessary resources, including computer time, people working on the project, or information you need to complete it. Then indicate that you are willing to make a contract with him or her within this period, if the boss can commit to you the resources necessary to do the job. This is straightforward, and something you can easily do. Everybody wins; nobody loses.

Negotiation is the key. What is the alternative? You can say nothing, grit your teeth, and work all weekend.

Team Negotiations

Team negotiations offer specific challenges. Whether on a formal negotiating team or with your boss, your spouse, or any number of stakeholders who want a seat at the table, team negotiations have several advantages and disadvantages (see Table 11.1).

General Guidelines

The same dynamics occur in a negotiation team as in any team performing a common task. There must be clarity and alignment on:

1. Negotiation goals and objectives.
2. Team roles and responsibilities.
3. Procedures and methods.
4. Relationships and negotiating styles.

Lack of alignment can create a nightmare for a negotiation team. Think about a time when you and your spouse disagreed on an issue one of your children wanted to negotiate. Or consider the sales manager who arrives in the negotiation and offers a key currency that the account executive has refused to concede. Working on a team to plan the negotiation, requires additional time to gain alignment on these key areas. Usually, the rule on planning for a team negotiation is: *Planning time increases exponentially with the size of the team.*

TABLE 11.1 Team Negotiations

Advantages	Disadvantages
Extra eyes and ears	Extra mouth
Planning with two heads	Need more time to plan
Someone manages the process, while others manage content	Dueling agendas
	Loose cannon
Buy-in during the negotiation	No single decision maker
Caucus more easily	Too many options
Real-time brainstorming	Role confusion/conflict
Divide responsibilities	

Gaining Alignment on Key Issues

In both planning and execution, team alignment on the previous four areas is crucial. Here are some considerations in each area:

Negotiation Goals and Objectives

- What are the objectives and desired outcomes for the team in this negotiation?
  —Business
  —Personal
- What are the key issues to be negotiated?
- What is our settlement range for each issue?
  —Opening position?
  —Desired settlement point?
  —Walk-away point?

Team Roles and Responsibilities

- Who will be involved in planning? Executing? Both?
- Who is the leader of the team?
- Who is designated as content expert?
- Who will run the negotiation session?
- Who has veto power? Or final authority?

Procedures and Methods

- Who will manage each stage of the negotiation?
- Who talks to the other side?
- What are the basic ground rules for the team?
- Based on the tactical orientation, how will the team approach this negotiation? Win-win? Adversarial? Neutral?
- What are the signals for caucusing? Taking a break? Moving to a new issue?
- What are the value and order of currencies and concessions?
- What are the nonnegotiables? Deal breakers?

- What is the form for the final agreement?
- Who and how will we manage implementation? Pitfalls? Missed items?

Relationships and Negotiating Styles

- What are the negotiating styles on our team? Theirs?
- Are there any personal issues within our team? With anyone on their team?
- How can we reconcile or manage these differences *before* the negotiation?

Even though there are many issues to settle within the team *before* you negotiate, using a team approach can help create collaboration and usually generates a better deal.

KEY POINTS

☞ In negotiating during buy and sell situations:
—Focus on value not on price.
—Develop the full value proposition.
—Continue to develop a broad-based customer relationship.

☞ In internal negotiations:
—Highlight areas of agreement at the beginning and throughout the negotiation.
—Convert the situation from a "me versus you" to an "us against the problem."
—Use facts and logic sparingly; if resistance occurs, use questioning and listening to understand the other party's point of view.
—Offer currencies beyond the issue being negotiated.
—Avoid overstating or inflating your wants and needs.
—Resist escalation.

☞ In negotiating with your boss:

—Break the task down into: *specification, time,* and *resources.*

—Use the concept of the triangle to estimate these factors.

—Remember the Rule of the Triangle—whenever adjustments are made to any of the sides, *the area must remain proportional.*

—Tips in handling a negotiation with your boss:

- Allow a reasonable time for a quality job.
- Determine the specifications.
- Build in a contingency reserve.
- Use resources creatively.
- Know which factor drives the project.
- Learn to say "Yes, and . . ." rather Than "No."
- In team negotiations:
  —Consider advantages and disadvantages.
  —The same dynamics occur in a negotiation team as in any team.
  —Planning time increases exponentially with the size of the team.
  —Check alignment on:
    - Negotiation goals and objectives.
    - Team roles and responsibilities.
    - Procedures and methods.
    - Relationships and negotiating styles.

Practical Application

Buy and Sell Negotiations

In negotiating during buy and sell situations:

- Focus on value not on price.
- Develop the full value proposition (see Figure 11.8).

How would I define the human and behavior impacts (HABI) to enhance the value proposition?

- Continue to develop a broad-based customer relationship.

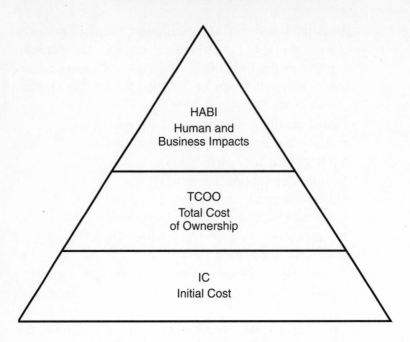

FIGURE 11.8 Value Proposition Pyramid

Who are the people in your customer's or vendor's organization who you could enlist to build a stronger bond between your organizations?

_____

_____

_____

Internal Negotiations

Who are the people in my customer organization who I rely on for resources?

_____

_____

_____

What resources (and other currencies) might I offer them to achieve my objectives?

_____

_____

_____

Negotiating with Your Boss

In negotiating with your boss:

- Break the task down into: *specification*, *time*, and *resources*.
- Use the concept of the triangle to estimate these factors.

The Triangle

Remember the Rule of the Triangle—whenever adjustments are made to any of the sides, *the area must remain proportional* (see Figure 11.9).

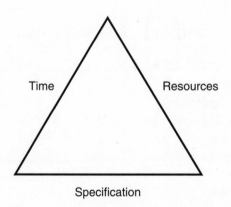

FIGURE 11.9   Specification-Time-Resources Triangle

Tips in Handling a Negotiation with Your Boss

- Allow a reasonable time for a quality job.
- Determine the specifications.
- Build in a contingency reserve.
- Use resources creatively.
- Know which *factor* drives the project.
- Learn to say "Yes, and . . ." rather Than "No."

Team Negotiations

Consider the advantages and disadvantages in Table 11.2. If the advantages outweigh the disadvantages, think about using a team approach.

Gaining Alignment on Key Issues

In both planning and execution, team alignment on the previous four areas is crucial. Here are some considerations in each area:

TABLE 11.2   Team Negotiations

Advantages	Disadvantages
Extra eyes and ears	Extra mouth
Planning with two heads	Need more time to plan
Someone manages the process, while others manage content	Dueling agendas
	Loose cannon
Buy-in during the negotiation	No single decision maker
Caucus more easily	Too many options
Real-time brainstorming	Role confusion/conflict
Divide responsibilities	

Negotiation Goals and Objectives

- What are the objectives and desired outcomes for the team in this negotiation?
  —Business
  —Personal
- What are the key issues to be negotiated?
- What is our settlement range for each issue?
  —Opening position?
  —Desired settlement point?
  —Walk-away point?

Notes:

Team Roles and Responsibilities

- Who will be involved in planning? Executing? Both?
- Who is the leader of the team?
- Who is designated as content expert?
- Who will run the negotiation session?
- Who has veto power? Or final authority?

Notes:

Procedures and Methods

- Who will manage each stage of the negotiation?
- Who talks to the other side?
- What are the basic ground rules for the team?
- Based on the tactical orientation, how will the team approach this negotiation? Win-win? Adversarial? Neutral?
- What are the signals for caucusing? Taking a break? Moving to a new issue?
- What are the value and order of currencies and concessions?

- What are the nonnegotiables? Deal breakers?
- What is the form for the final agreement?
- Who and how will we manage implementation? Pitfalls? Missed items?

Notes:

Relationships and Negotiating Styles

- What are the negotiating styles on our team? Theirs?
- Are there any personal issues within our team? With anyone on their team?
- How can we reconcile or manage these differences *before* the negotiation?

Notes:

Putting It All Together

He who knows only his own side of the case, knows little of that.

—John Stuart Mill (1806–1873)
British philosopher and economist

Practical Negotiating:
Planning Guide—Annotated

In Section One of this book, we worked through the planning phase of negotiating. In Section Two, we explored how to execute a negotiation. Now, let's put it all together into an operational framework. The annotated *Planning Guide* provided in this chapter gives you an opportunity to apply all the skills from the book to a specific negotiation. Appendix B contains a *Planning Guide* without the annotation for your reproduction and use in future negotiations.

As you use this guide, keep in mind that you can carefully plan your side, but you may have to speculate about the other side. Good luck!

Step 1: Determine Wants and Needs

Remember that identifying and satisfying the underlying needs of both parties represents the essence of the negotiation process (see Table 12.1). Can both parties' needs be satisfied? Yes, if they both explore beneath the surface. Think of some questions you might ask to reveal the other side's underlying needs. If you are not sure, review the material in Chapter 2.

Create a Needs/Objectives Matrix
To fill in the boxes in Table 12.2, ask yourself: "What am I trying to accomplish in this negotiation?" and "What is the other side trying

TABLE 12.1 Wants and Needs

Your Side	Other Side
What do you want?	*What do they want?*
What would getting this (want) do for you?	*What would getting this (want) do for them?*
Is this my need? If you're not sure, ask the question again: What would getting this do for you?	*Is this their need? If you're not sure, ask the question again: What would getting this do for them?*

to accomplish?" The answers help identify your negotiation objectives, but don't stop there. Distinguish business (or substantive) and personal objectives, by asking yourself, "What are my personal objectives? Theirs?" Remember the test: If you can substitute another person (on your side or theirs) and the need remains, then the need is business rather than personal. Review the list and circle the objectives that are most critical.

TABLE 12.2 Needs/Objectives Matrix

Needs/ Objectives	Your Side	Other Side
Business		
Personal		

Step 2: Position Development

In a specific negotiation, needs and objectives tend to remain constant, but positions change. Every negotiation involves one or more issues. Plan a settlement range for each.

Start with the desired settlement point, decide on an opening position, and then establish your walk-away point (see Figure 12.1).

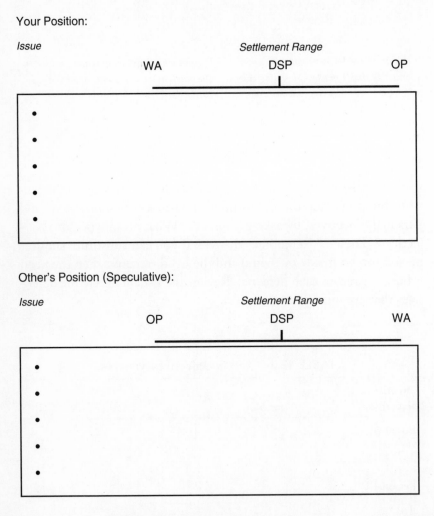

FIGURE 12.1 Position Development

Step 3: Currencies/Options

Currencies are essential to the negotiation process (see Table 12.3). To determine which currencies you might offer, consider what you know about their needs and what currencies you might offer to meet those needs. Be sure to determine the "street value" of the currencies you offer. To predict what they might offer, consider your needs and what currencies they could offer to meet those needs. Remember the three currency types: prime, alternative, and elegant. In Chapter 4, we expanded your view on currencies and provided some guidance on how to make concessions.

TABLE 12.3 Currencies/Options

Your Side	Other Side
Considering what you know about their needs, what currencies might you offer to meet those needs?	Considering my needs, what currencies might they offer to meet those needs?
•	•
•	•
•	•
•	•
•	•

Step 4: Power Assessment

In negotiation, *power is a function of alternatives*. Think about alternatives in three categories: (1) sources, (2) currencies, and (3) skills (see Table 12.4). Don't overlook the power of the relationship and how this contributes to a true win-win agreement. Refer to Chapter 5 for more information on enhancing your power.

TABLE 12.4   Power Assessment

Your Side	Other Side
Alternative sources	*Alternative sources*
•	•
•	•
•	•
•	•
Alternative currencies (check one)	*Alternative currencies (check one)*
☐ Plenty available to close the gap	☐ Plenty available to close the gap
☐ Sufficient to close the gap	☐ Sufficient to close the gap
☐ Need to generate/explore	☐ Need to generate/explore
Alternative skills	*Alternative skills*
•	•
•	•
•	•
•	•

Step 5: Planning to Execute Stages

The Negotiation Stages Model serves as a road map during the negotiation, but it can also serve you well during the planning phase (see Table 12.5). If you are negotiating as a team, this framework is essential to ensuring a smooth process. As we learned in Chapter 6, this is both a micro model to be followed in a single meeting and a macro model to orient you during an extended negotiation.

TABLE 12.5   Negotiation Stages Model

Stages	Critical Tasks
Opening	Set the climate and agenda.
	Establish the process.
	State and respond to opening positions.
Notes:	
Exploring	Distinguish between wants and needs.
	Identify alternative currencies/options.
	Match currencies to needs.
Notes:	
Closing	Summarize the agreement and contract.
	Communicate and implement.
Notes:	

Step 6: Assessing Your Negotiating Styles

The *Negotiation Style Survey* is found in Appendix A. As we noted in Chapter 7, your negotiation style refers to your general approach or behavioral style in negotiating. Even though you have a specific style, you can expand your repertoire by practicing the key skills. In planning your negotiation, it's desirable to review your negotiating style versus the style of the other side. With a team, talk about your negotiating styles and whether they complement or clash.

TABLE 12.6 Negotiating Style Survey

Your Side	Other Side
Names:	*Names:*
•	•
•	•
•	•
•	•
•	•
Negotiating style (check those that apply):	*Negotiating style* (check those that apply):
☐ Aggressive/Confronting	☐ Aggressive/Confronting
☐ Assertive/Persuasive	☐ Assertive/Persuasive
☐ Open/Responsive	☐ Open/Responsive
☐ Avoiding/Withdrawing	☐ Avoiding/Withdrawing

Step 7: Determine Your Tactical Orientation

Tactical orientation refers to a process that provides you with general guidance in selecting tactics consistent with your objectives and intent (see Table 12.7). You should be fairly sure of your answers and able to speculate about those of the other side. If you are not sure of some of their answers, you can use these questions early in the negotiation process to determine what zone they are in.

TABLE 12.7 Tactical Orientation Process

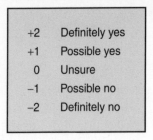

+2	Definitely yes
+1	Possible yes
0	Unsure
−1	Possible no
−2	Definitely no

- Do I trust them? _____
- Am I under time pressure? _____
- Is reaching a win/win agreement desirable? _____
- Am I open to alternative outcomes? _____
- Do I want a long-term relationship? _____

My Score: _____

Do they trust me? _____
Are they? _____
To them? _____
Are they? _____
Do they? _____

Their Score: _____

Win/Win	Neutral	Adversarial

+10   +8   +6   +4   +2   0   −2   −4   −6   −8   −10

- In which "Zone" am I? _____
- In which "Zone" are they? _____

Step 8: Tactical Selection

Once you've determined your side and the other's tactical orientation, you can assess the tactics that they are likely to use (see Table 12.8). Consider the history with the other party, or even the experience of initiating this negotiation. Are they easy or difficult to deal with on issues such as scheduling and sharing information? If they are likely to use adversarial zone tactics, determine what win-win zone tactics you might use. Consult Chapters 8 and 9 for additional guidance.

TABLE 12.8 Tactics by Stage

Stage	Win-Win Zone Tactics	Adversarial Zone Tactics
Opening		
Set the climate and agenda	Agenda	Missing man maneuver
	Common interests	Deadline pressure
Establish the process	Disclosure	Personal attacks
State and respond to opening positions	Authority limits	Rules
	Team seating	Good guy/Bad guy
	Columbo	Red herring
	Objective criteria	Poor mouthing
	Saying no	Crunch time
	Walk-Away	Nonnegotiable demands
Exploring		
Distinguish between wants and needs	Create empathy	Bluffing/Lying
	Expand the pie	Cherry-picking
Identify alternative currencies/options	Scaling	Divide and conquer
	Testing questions	End run
Match currencies to needs	Brainstorming	Funny money
	Bundling	Split the difference
	What if . . .?	Surprises
	Balancing the scales	Take it or leave it
	Concessions	Threats
	Patience/Persistence	
	Soak time	
	Warn, don't threaten	
	Zeroing in	
Closing		
Summarize the agreement and contract	Caucus	Authority escalation
	Change of pace	Deadlock
Communicate and implement	Closing the deal	Fait accompli
	Mark up the document	Last and final offer
	Pinch factor	Nibbling
	Side memos	Simple solutions
	Summarizing	Split the difference

KEY PRINCIPLES OF PRACTICAL NEGOTIATING

Let us never negotiate out of fear, but let us never fear to negotiate.
—John F. Kennedy, Inaugural Address, January 20, 1961

As I was finishing the book, I realized something was missing. On reflection, I thought about similar books that I admired and discovered that all had a common characteristic—a set of key principles. So here are 12 principles to keep in mind when negotiating:

1. Conflict is inevitable! Therefore, negotiation is a survival skill than can be learned.
2. Negotiate from *need* not *greed.* Strive for a win-win outcome.
3. If you must, compromise on your *wants*, but not on your *needs.*
4. Be aware of both *business* (substantive) and *personal* needs in the negotiation.
5. Develop a settlement range including:
   - Desired settlement point
   - Opening position
   - Walk-away point
6. Be creative in developing currencies and use them to add value to the deal.
7. Concessions are essential to the give-and-take process of negotiating. Watch how you make them.
8. In negotiation, *power* is a function of *alternatives:*
   - Alternative sources
   - Alternative currencies
   - Alternative skills
9. Use the Negotiation Stages Model as a road map.
10. Be aware of your negotiation style. Use the key skills to expand your repertoire.

11. Assess your (and the other's) tactical orientation.
12. Choose the best tactics to accomplish your objectives. Every behavior communicates.

Conclusion

Negotiation provides the most effective method for conflict resolution because it actively involves the parties in the process. As we saw in the examples used in this book and those we witness everyday in the news, opportunities to negotiate surround us. Whether in our nations, organizations, businesses, or families, conflict exists. It's up to us to choose the best way to resolve it and to encourage others to participate.

Good luck!

APPENDIX

A

Negotiation Style Survey

The most difficult thing in life is to know yourself.
— Thales, ancient Greek philosopher

Instructions

The Negotiation Style Survey is designed to provide you with an assessment of your preferred negotiating style. There are no right or wrong answers. Respond to each item based on the way you really react, rather than how you would like to react.

Allocate *10 points* among the four alternative answers for each of the 12 items in the survey. Award the largest number of points to your most likely reaction to the situation as illustrated in the following example:

1. When the other party does something that irritates me, my tendency is to:

Use strong, direct language and tell the person to stop.	Try to persuade the person to stop.	Listen and disclose my feelings.	Say and do nothing.
2	5	3	0

Be certain that your answers add up to 10.

Source: Adapted from *Conflict-Management Style Survey*, Marc Robert, The Pfeiffer & Company Library CD-ROM, by J. William Pfeiffer, Editor, Copyright 1996, by Pfeiffer & Company, San Diego, CA. Reprinted with permission of John Wiley & Sons, Inc.

1. I approach negotiation situations as:

Adversarial—us versus them.	Competitive— each side working to get its needs met.	Collaborative— both sides working together to resolve differences.	To be avoided whenever possible.
_____	_____	_____	_____

2. When the other party does something that irritates me, my tendency is to:

Use strong, direct language and tell the person to stop.	Try to persuade the person to stop.	Listen and disclose my feelings.	Say and do nothing.
_____	_____	_____	_____

3. In general, when I negotiate with the other party, I tend to:

Take a firm position.	Explain the merits of my position.	Respond by asking questions.	Remain passive and see what happens.
_____	_____	_____	_____

4. When I perceive the other party as meeting his or her needs at my expense, I am apt to:

Confront the other party and insist that he or she change the situation.	Rely on reason and facts when attempting to resolve the situation.	Explore other alternatives, options, and so on.	Accept the situation as it is.
_____	_____	_____	_____

5. When involved in a difficult negotiation, my general pattern is to:

Firmly state and maintain my position.	Examine the issues as logically as possible.	Search for a workable compromise.	Let the problems resolve themselves over time.
_____	_____	_____	_____

(continued)

6. When asked to make a concession late in the negotiation, I tend to:

Hold firmly.	Only make the concession if it is reciprocated.	Ask the other party if this would close the deal.	Offer the concession unilaterally.
_____	_____	_____	_____

7. Following a serious disagreement with the other person, I:

Strongly desire to go back and settle things my way.	Want to go back and work it out—using whatever give and take is necessary	Schedule another meeting to probe for the real issues.	Let it lie and not plan to initiate further contact.
_____	_____	_____	_____

8. When the other party criticizes me or my company on an issue such as technical quality, price, and so on, I tend to:

Forcefully defend my company's position.	Use facts or evidence to prove my point.	Probe to surface the underlying objection.	Change the subject.
_____	_____	_____	_____

9. The feedback that I receive from most people about how I behave when negotiating is that I:

Take a hard stance to get my way.	Try to work out differences cooperatively.	Am easygoing and take a soft or conciliatory position.	Usually avoid the situation.
_____	_____	_____	_____

10. When communicating with the other party in a negotiation, I:

Try to overpower the other person by monopolizing the conversation.	Talk a little bit more than I listen.	Am an active listener (feeding back words and feelings).	Am a passive listener (agreeing and apologizing).
_____	_____	_____	_____

11. In responding to adversarial tactics, I tend to:

Respond in kind to the other party.	Acknowledge the tactic and try to convince the other party to stop.	Keep my cool and wait for opportunities to intervene.	Make a concession to appease the other party.
_____	_____	_____	_____

12. I perceive my negotiation style as:

Persistent	Determined	Personable	Risk averse
Tough-minded	Orderly	Approachable	Cautious
Dominating	Logical	Open	Compromising
Decisive	Vigilant	Flexible	Noncommittal
_____	_____	_____	_____

Add the columns and display the results here:

_____	_____	_____	$\dfrac{\rule{2cm}{0.4pt}}{\text{A/W}} = 120$
A/C	A/P	O/R	

Column Analysis

A/C = Aggressive/Confronting
High scores indicate a strong need to control situations and/or people. Described as persistent, tough-minded, dominating, and decisive.

A/P = Assertive/Persuasive
High scores indicate a direct approach using facts and logic to defend positions. Described as determined, persuasive and logical, and willing to collaborate.

O/R = Open/Responsive
High scores indicate a tendency to be open and listen carefully, to ask questions and respond regarding needs and issues. Described as open and flexible, conciliatory, approachable, and seeking to understand.

A/W = Avoiding/Withdrawing
High scores indicate a tendency to avoid confrontation, even to the point of withdrawal. Described as risk averse, cautious, and compromising.

(continued)

Additional Analysis

$$A/C + A/P = A \text{ Score} \underline{\hspace{3cm}}$$

$$O/R + A/W = B \text{ Score} \underline{\hspace{3cm}}$$

If your A score is significantly higher (20+ points), you tend toward a Push (Aggressive/Assertive style).

If your B score is significantly higher (20+ points), you tend toward a Pull (Collaborative/Passive style).

Practical Negotiating: Planning Guide

Step 1: Determine Wants and Needs

TABLE B.1 Wants and Needs

Your Side	Other Side
What do you want?	*What do they want?*
What would getting this (want) do for you?	*What would getting this (want) do for them?*
Is this my need? If you're not sure, ask the question again. What would getting this do for you?	*Is this their need? If you're not sure, ask the question again. What would getting this do for them?*

Create a Needs/Objectives Matrix

TABLE B.2 Needs/Objectives Matrix

Needs/ Objectives	Your Side	Other Side
Business		
Personal		

Step 2: Position Development

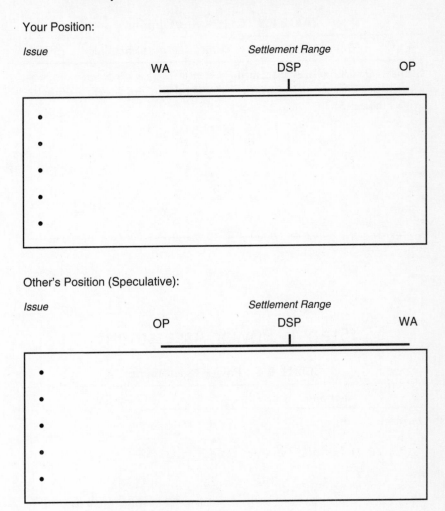

FIGURE B.1 Position Development

Step 3: Currencies/Options

TABLE B.3   Currencies/Options

Your Side	Other Side
Considering what you know about their needs, what currencies might you offer to meet those needs?	Considering my needs, what currencies might they offer to meet those needs?
•	•
•	•
•	•
•	•
•	•

Step 4: Power Assessment

TABLE B.4   Power Assessment

Your Side	Other Side
Alternative sources	*Alternative sources*
•	•
•	•
•	•
Alternative currencies (check one)	*Alternative currencies (check one)*
☐ Plenty available to close the gap	☐ Plenty available to close the gap
☐ Sufficient to close the gap	☐ Sufficient to close the gap
☐ Need to generate/explore	☐ Need to generate/explore
Alternative skills	*Alternative skills*
•	•
•	•
•	•

Step 5: Planning to Execute Stages

TABLE B.5 Negotiation Stages Model

Stages	Critical Tasks
Opening	Set the climate and agenda.
	Establish the process.
	State and respond to opening positions.
Notes:	
Exploring	Distinguish between wants and needs.
	Identify alternative currencies/options.
	Match currencies to needs.
Notes:	
Closing	Summarize the agreement and contract.
	Communicate and implement.
Notes:	

Step 6: Assessing Your Negotiating Styles

TABLE B.6 Negotiating Style Survey

Your Side	Other Side
Names:	*Names:*
•	•
•	•
•	•
Negotiating style	*Negotiating style*
(check those that apply):	(check those that apply):
☐ Aggressive/Confronting	☐ Aggressive/Confronting
☐ Assertive/Persuasive	☐ Assertive/Persuasive
☐ Open/Responsive	☐ Open/Responsive
☐ Avoiding/Withdrawing	☐ Avoiding/Withdrawing

Step 7: Determine Your Tactical Orientation

TABLE B.7 Tactical Orientation Process

+2	Definitely yes
+1	Possible yes
0	Unsure
−1	Possible no
−2	Definitely no

- Do I trust them? _____ Do they trust me? _____
- Am I under time pressure? _____ Are they? _____
- Is reaching a win/win agreement desirable? _____ To them? _____
- Am I open to alternative outcomes? _____ Are they? _____
- Do I want a long-term relationship? _____ Do they? _____

My Score: _____ Their Score: _____

Win/Win   Neutral   Adversarial

+10 +8 +6 +4 +2 0 −2 −4 −6 −8 −10

- In which "Zone" am I? _____
- In which "Zone" are they? _____

Step 8: Tactical Selection

TABLE B.8   Tactics by Stage

Stage	Win-Win Zone Tactics	Adversarial Zone Tactics
Opening		
Set the climate and agenda	Agenda	Missing man maneuver
	Common interests	Deadline pressure
Establish the process	Disclosure	Personal attacks
State and respond to opening positions	Authority limits	Rules
	Team seating	Good guy/Bad guy
	Columbo	Red herring
	Objective criteria	Poor mouthing
	Saying no	Crunch time
	Walk-Away	Nonnegotiable demands
Exploring		
Distinguish between wants and needs	Create empathy	Bluffing/Lying
	Expand the pie	Cherry-picking
Identify alternative currencies/options	Scaling	Divide and conquer
	Testing questions	End run
Match currencies to needs	Brainstorming	Funny money
	Bundling	Split the difference
	What if . . .?	Surprises
	Balancing the scales	Take it or leave it
	Concessions	Threats
	Patience/Persistence	
	Soak time	
	Warn, don't threaten	
	Zeroing in	
Closing		
Summarize the agreement and contract	Caucus	Authority escalation
	Change of pace	Deadlock
Communicate and implement	Closing the deal	Fait accompli
	Mark up the document	Last and final offer
	Pinch factor	Nibbling
	Side memos	Simple solutions
	Summarizing	Split the difference

Notes

Chapter 1

1. Deborah M. Kolb, "Will You Thrive or Just Survive?" *Negotiation Newsletter* (Harvard Business School Publishing, January, 2005).
2. When I introduce this model in workshops, I often joke that it is so old that it was chiseled on the other side of the Ten Commandments. In fact, the reference I found was nineteenth century. Elias St. Elmo Lewis proposed the first effects model named the AIDA model—which stands for Attention, Interest, Desire, and Action—in 1898. The model described the sequential process that consumers must go through to make a purchase. By 1925, the model had become so prevalent, it was estimated that 90 percent of the persons engaged in selling were influenced by either the AIDA model or one of its variations. I changed Desire to Decision to make the model more appropriate to negotiation, and Action to Implementation since Action implies transactional selling while Implementation infers a longer process for the transfer of goods and services.

Chapter 2

1. *Chariots of Fire*, a movie written by Colin Welland, directed by Hugh Hudson (Warner Bros., 1981).
2. James K. Sebenius, "What Divides You May Unite You," *Negotiation Newsletter,* July 2005, p. 5.

Chapter 3

1. The Needs/Objectives Matrix is an adaptation of the concepts of "Windows of Interest" in *Value Added Negotiating: The Breakthrough Method for Building Balanced Deals* by Karl and Steve Albrecht (Homewood, IL: Business One Irwin, 1993).

Chapter 4

1. This description of currencies has been cited throughout the literature. However, the term *elegant*—currencies of low cost to the provider but high value to the receiver—is also referred to as of "minimal complication and maximum impact." *Positive Negotiation Program* (Nashua, NH: Situation Management Systems, 1991), pp. 1–26.
2. A version of this exercise is also used in the *Positive Negotiation Program* (Nashua, NH: Situation Management Systems, 1991), pp. 3–5.
3. Karl Albrecht and Steve Albrecht, *Added Value Negotiating: The Breakthrough Method for Building Balanced Deals* (Homewood, IL: Business One Irwin, 1993), p. 44.
4. Adapted from Tom Reilly, *Value-Added Selling Techniques: How to Sell More Profitably, Confidently, and Professionally*, 2nd ed. (New York: McGraw-Hill, 2002), and *Value-Added Sales Management* (New York: McGraw-Hill, 1993).
5. Roger Fisher and William Ury, *Getting to Yes: Negotiating Agreements without Giving In* (New York: Penguin Books, 1983). BATNA is an acronym for "Best Alternative to a Negotiated Agreement" with the other party. In other words, if I can't reach an agreement with you, what other options or choices do I have?

Chapter 5

1. Roger Dawson, author of *Secrets of Power Negotiating*, in promotional material for his seminars.
2. Herb Cohen, *You Can Negotiate Anything* (New York: Bantam, 1983).
3. Roger Fisher and William Ury, *Getting to Yes: Negotiating Agreement without Giving In*, 2nd ed. (New York: Penguin Books, 1991), p. 179.

Chapter 6

1. At the time I worked with him, Lester B. Wolff was an attorney with the Home Owners Warranty. He is now involved with Construction Arbitration Services.
2. Robert C. Bordone and Gillien S. Todd, "Have You Negotiated How You'll Negotiate?" *Negotiation Newsletter,* September, 2005, p. 7.

Chapter 7

1. Adapted from Terry Bacon, *Interpersonal and Interactive Skills Workshop* (Durango, CO: LORE International Institute, 1995).
2. This model is an adaptation of the work of William S. Swan, PhD, specifically the "Conflict Interaction Analysis" model that appears in *How to Do a Superior Performance Appraisal* (New York: John Wiley & Sons, 1991).
3. David Berlew, author of the *Positive Power and Influence* and the *Positive Negotiation Programs* (Nashua, NH: Situation Management Systems).
4. Roger Fisher and William Ury, *Getting to Yes: Negotiating Agreement without Giving In*, 2nd ed. (New York: Penguin Books, 1991).

Chapter 8

1. Roger Fisher and William Ury, *Getting to Yes: Negotiating Agreement without Giving In*, 2nd ed. (New York: Penguin Books, 1991).
2. Chester L. Karrass, *Give and Take: The Complete Guide to Negotiating Strategies and Tactics*, rev. ed. (New York: Harper Business, 1974/1993), p. 145.

Chapter 9

1. Karl Albrecht and Steve Albrecht, *Added Value Negotiating: The Breakthrough Method for Building Balanced Deals* (Homewood, IL: Business One Irwin, 1993).
2. Gavin Kennedy, Essential Negotiation (*Economist Newspaper*, 2004).
3. Roger Dawson, *Secrets of Power Negotiating*, 2nd ed. (Franklin Lakes, NJ: Career Press, 2001).
4. Roger Fisher and William Ury, *Getting to Yes: Negotiating Agreement without Giving In*, 2nd ed. (New York: Penguin Books, 1991).
5. Chester L. Karrass coined the term *Krunch* to describe a similar tactic in *Give and Take: The Complete Guide to Negotiating Strategies and Tactics*, rev. ed. (New York: Harper Business, 1974/1993), p. 93.

Chapter 11

1. The concept of human and business impacts (HABI), was developed by Paul Hafner and Dan Blitzer, in the Fundamentals of Lighting

Workshop, offered through the Philips Lighting Company's Lighting Application Center, Somerset, NJ, 2006.

2. Terry Bacon, *Selling to Major Account* (New York: AMACOM, 1999), p. 190.
3. David Bradford and Allan Cohen, *Influence without Authority* (New York: John Wiley & Sons, 1989).
4. The concept of "hallway negotiations" was coined by David Berlew in the *Positive Negotiation Program* (Nashua, NH: Situation Management Systems, 1991), p. 6–1.
5. A version of this material was published previously by Tom Gosselin, "Negotiating with Your Boss" in *Training and Development Magazine* (May, 1993), pp. 37–40.

Bibliography

Albrecht, Karl, and Steve Albrecht. *Added Value Negotiating: The Break-through Method for Building Balanced Deals.* Homewood, IL: Business One Irwin, 1993.

Alessandra, Tony, Phil Wexler, and Rick Barrera. *Non-Manipulative Selling.* New York: Prentice-Hall Press, 1987.

Bacon, Terry. *Interpersonal and Interactive Skills Workshop.* Lore International Institute, Durango, CO, 1995.

Bacon, Terry. *Selling to Major Accounts.* New York: AMACOM, 1999.

Berlew, David. *Positive Negotiation Program.* Nashua, NH: Situation Management Systems, 1991, p. 6-1.

Berlew, David. *Positive Power and Influence.* Nashua, NH: Situation Management Systems, 1991.

Bordone, Robert C., and Gillien S. Todd. "Have You Negotiated How You'll Negotiate?" *Negotiation Newsletter,* September 2005, p. 7.

Cohen, Allan, and David Bradford. *Influence without Authority.* New York: John Wiley & Sons, 1989.

Cohen, Herb. *You Can Negotiate Anything.* New York: Bantam Books, 1983.

Dawson, Roger. *Secrets of Power Negotiating.* 2nd ed. Franklin Lakes, NJ: Career Press, 2001.

Fisher, Roger, and William Ury (with Bruce Patton). *Getting to Yes: Negotiating Agreement without Giving In.* 2nd ed. New York: Penguin Books, 1991.

Freund, James C. *Smart Negotiating: How to Make Good Deals in the Real World.* New York: Fireside, 1992.

Gosselin, Tom. "Negotiating with Your Boss," *Training and Development Magazine* (May 1993).

Guder, Robert F. *Negotiating Techniques.* Los Altos, CA: Crisp Publications, 1988.

Karrass, Chester L. *Give and Take: The Complete Guide to Negotiating Strategies and Tactics.* New York: Thomas Y. Crowell, 1974/1993.

Keiser, Thomas C. "Negotiating with a Customer You Can't Afford to Lose," *Harvard Business Review*, 88, no. 6 (1988), pp. 30–34.

Kennedy, Gavin. "Essential Negotiation," *Economist Newspaper* (2004).

Kolb, Deborah M. "Will You Thrive or Just Survive?" *Negotiation Newsletter,* January 2005.

Koren, Leonard, and Peter Goodman. *The Haggler's Handbook.* New York: W.W. Norton, 1991.

Lewicki, Roy J., and Joseph A. Litterer. *Negotiation.* Homewood, IL: Irwin, 1985.

Lum, Grande. *The Negotiation Fieldbook: Simple Strategies to Help You Negotiate Everything.* New York: McGraw-Hill, 2005.

Nierenberg, Gerard I. *Fundamentals of Negotiating.* New York: Hawthorne Books, 1973.

Reilly, Tom. *Value-Added Selling Techniques: How to Sell More Profitably, Confidently, and Professionally.* 2nd ed. New York: McGraw-Hill, 2002.

Reilly, Tom, *Value-Added Sales Management.* New York: McGraw-Hill, 1993.

Sebenius, James K. "What Divides You May Unite You," *Negotiation Newsletter,* July 2005, p. 5.

Shapiro, Ronald M., and Mark A. Jankowski. *The Power of Nice: How to Negotiate So Everyone Wins—Especially You.* rev. ed. New York: John Wiley & Sons, 2001, p. 3.

Sperber, Philip. *Fail-Safe Business Negotiations.* Englewood Cliffs, NJ: Prentice-Hall, 1983.

Stark, Peter B., and Jane Flaherty. *The Only Negotiating Guide You'll Ever Need: 101 Ways to Win Every Time in Any Situation.* New York: Broadway Books, 2003.

Swan, William S. *How to Do a Superior Performance Appraisal.* New York: John Wiley & Sons, 1991.

Ury, William. *Getting Past No: Negotiating with Difficult People.* New York: Bantam Books, 1991.

Volkema, Roger J. *The Negotiation Tool Kit: How to Get Exactly What You Want in Any Business or Personal Situation.* New York: AMACOM, 1999.

Index

225